1 MONTH OF
FREE
READING

at

www.ForgottenBooks.com

By purchasing this book you are eligible for one month membership to ForgottenBooks.com, giving you unlimited access to our entire collection of over 1,000,000 titles via our web site and mobile apps.

To claim your free month visit:
www.forgottenbooks.com/free518687

ISBN 978-0-484-07348-6
PIBN 10518687

OF THE

DONORS AND FOUNDERS

OF THE

Theological Seminary

OF THE

PROTESTANT EPISCOPAL CHURCH

IN THE DIOCESE OF OHIO,

AND

KENYON COLLEGE;

BEING THE REPORT OF A COMMITTEE OF THE BOARD
OF TRUSTEES, PRESENTED SEPT. 27, 1860.

―――〜〜〜●〜〜〜―――

CINCINNATI:
MOORE, WILSTACH, KEYS & CO., PRINTERS,
25 WEST FOURTH STREET.
1860.

KENYON COLLEGE.

Middleton, Strobridge & Co. Lith Cin. O.

OF THE

DONORS AND FOUNDERS

OF THE

THEOLOGICAL SEMINARY

OF THE

PROTESTANT EPISCOPAL CHURCH

IN THE DIOCESE OF OHIO,

AND

KENYON COLLEGE;

BEING THE REPORT OF A COMMITTEE OF THE BOARD
OF TRUSTEES, PRESENTED SEPT. 27, 1860.

CINCINNATI:
MOORE, WILSTACH, KEYS & CO., Printers,
25 WEST FOURTH STREET.
1860.

MEMENTO.

To the Board of Trustees of the Theological Seminary of the Protestant Episcopal Church in the Diocese of Ohio.

Gentlemen :

Having been appointed a committee to prepare for publication a statement of donations made to our Diocesan Institutions, the following is respectfully submitted.   S. A. Bronson. *

To the Donors of the Theological Seminary and Kenyon College.

Dear Friends :

As you have generously parted with the fruits of your toil, and many of you have denied self, and abridged personal comforts to advance an institution devoted to religion and learning, which you are perhaps never to see, it is supposable that you may sometimes inquire what has been done with those gifts? Has good been effected ; is their value still preserved to bless coming ages ; or have they been unwisely wasted or lavishly squandered for the personal gratification of individuals? Has the purpose of so frequent appeals for funds been legitimate, and to supply reasonable wants, or to remedy the effects of bad management? Has the Institution arisen to any thing that promises to be a credit to its founders and a blessing to the Church? Have not the funds contributed been vastly out of proportion to the results ?

The following view will, it is hoped, return an adequate reply to these and all questions that may be asked. Most will probably find that less has been given, less lost by mistake and bad management, and that the present position of the Institution, as to appliances and

---

* t my request two others, the Rt. Rev. G. T. Bedell, D. D., and Pres't. Lorin Andrews, LL. D., were added to the Committee, to whom the whole has been submitted for revision.

facilities for instruction, and its prospect of growth and perma-
nency, are better, than is supposed. A friend was asked, not long
since, after viewing the buildings, making acquaintance with the
officers, and visiting them at their houses, "How much had been
given to these Institutions?" His answer was, more than double
the actual amount. If such impressions are common, it is time they
were corrected by a statement of facts.

This report, however, was suggested by a desire to offer a token
of gratitude to the Donors. Probably no institutions, of the importance and extent of these, have ever been built up by the gifts
of so many, or nourished by so many praying hearts. May
Heaven's richest blessings crown them all, is the prayer of him who
writes this, and of the Board which he represents.

The first move ever made by Episcopalians, in Ohio, to apply to
Eastern Churches for aid to our Western frontier, was in a sugges-
tion of Bishop Chase, in his address to the Convention of the
Diocese, in 1821. After noticing the destitution of Ohio, and the
hopelessness of any supply, without special effort, Bishop C. urged
three points for the consideration of the Convention:

1. The formation of a Diocesan Missionary Society.

2. That an address be presented to Eastern Bishops and Churches,
asking pecuniary aid.

3. The appointment of a day of fasting and prayer.

In accordance with these suggestions, a Society was formed, of
which the Bishop was President; the Rev. R. Searle, Vice-Presi-
dent; Rev. Samuel Johnston, Recording Secretary; Rev. P. Chase,
Jr., Corresponding Secretary; and B. Gardiner, Esq., Treasurer.
The last Friday in August was set apart as a day of fasting and
prayer, and the Rev. P. Chase, Jr., was appointed an agent to apply
to Eastern Churches for aid.

The result of this application was the collection of $2,911 09.
This sum, for a number of years, afforded important aid in the support of missionaries throughout the wide wilderness of Ohio.

From this movement, and its results, two facts were ascertained
by the Church in Ohio:

1. That foreign aid could be had by asking.

2. That money to support missionaries would be of but little use
unless men could be found.

Meanwhile, Bishop Chase's address to the Ohio Convention

reached England. In the British *Critic*, for May, 1822, appeared the following notice of the Journal of the Ohio Convention, written by the Rev. Thomas Hartwell Horne :

" Bishop Chase traveled, in the course of the year 1820, on horseback (which is the only way of visiting infant settlements of that country), a distance of 1271 miles." Other remarks followed (bringing the condition and wants of Ohio very fully before the British public), founded particularly upon the appeal of the Church in Ohio for missionary assistance.

Bishop Chase says : " It was these representations in the British Critic, noticed by his son in an American newspaper, and reported by him to his father, which kindled hope in their almost despairing minds, and led to a determination to visit a country where their wants in the Western wilderness were thus known and pitied." It was then determined that as money did not succeed in bringing missionaries to the West, an institution of learning must be provided for their education.

Accordingly, in the year 1823, the Rev. Philander Chase, Jr., was appointed Agent, to visit England and apply for further aid. He was authorized to draw upon the funds of the Missionary Society of Ohio for his salary and expenses. But the health of this promising young man so rapidly failed, that he was unable to proceed.

Now it was that Bishop Chase himself determined to go to England ; and accordingly started, August 4, 1823. He was favored by the Hon. Henry Clay with a letter of introduction to the Right Hon. Admiral Lord Gambier. These two statesmen had met as commissioners at the treaty of Ghent, in 1815, and by means of their acquaintance Bishop Chase was at once introduced to some of the most prominent and influential men in England. After the way was prepared, and the object of his visit fully understood, he proceeded to execute a conditional deed of his farm at Worthington, valued by him at $5000, to trustees in England, viz : Lords Kenyon and Gambier, the Rev. Geo. Gaskin, D. D., and Henry Hoare, Esq., as a foundation for a Theological Seminary. Upon this farm the Seminary was to be built, unless some other place should be offered, which the Hon. Henry Clay should esteem equally valuable. Should such a place be offered this deed was to be void.

The above-named Trustees then issued the following : " *Appeal in Behalf of the Diocese of Ohio, in the Western Territory of the United States :"*

"The Episcopal Church of the United States of America derives its origin from this country. Ten dioceses have been formed, nine of which are in the Atlantic States, east of the Allegany Mountains. Portions of two of these dioceses, those of Philadelphia and Virginia, reach across the mountains, as they are co-extensive with the respective States of Pennsylvania and Virginia ; but the diocese of Ohio is the only diocese yet formed beyond those mountains in the Western Territory of the States.

" The pressing want of clergymen in this diocese has led the Rt. Rev. Prelate, who has the care of its scattered parishes, to visit this country, that he may procure that aid which is necessary to preserve this infant Church from perishing, and which he had no hopes of procuring elsewhere.

" The Hon. Henry Clay, Speaker of the House of Representatives of the United States, himself an inhabitant of the State of Kentucky, in the Western Territory, and perfectly acquainted with the destitute condition of that Territory, in respect of Christian ministers and sacred ordinances, addressed a letter to the Right Hon. Admiral Lord Gambier, requesting his lordship's assistance in promoting the object of Bishop Chase's visit to this country.

" Lord Gambier having introduced the subject to some of his friends well acquainted with the constitution and proceedings of the American Episcopal Church, they entered into a full examination of the claims of the Diocese of Ohio on Christian benevolence, and the expediency of rendering the aid requested. The result has been their full conviction that the spiritual wants of that diocese call for special provision and assistance, and that appropriate and adequate provision for the supply of such wants requires the establishment of an institution on the spot, in which natives of the country may be prepared for the ministry at an expense within their reach, and in habits suited to the sphere of their labors ; and they are satisfied that this important object is not likely to be accomplished without liberal aid from this country."

Here the "Appeal " proceeds to state the grounds of their convictions, which it is not necessary here to repeat, and in conclusion says :

"The powerful appeal which these facts make to the benevolent heart will not, as the friends of Bishop Chase are persuaded, be made in vain. Adequate aid, furnished at this juncture, will consolidate and extend the efficiency of the American Church, by contributing to supply with suitable ministers that vast mass of population which is continually emigrating westward; while without such aid the Church itself, established by such a course of self-denying and unwearied toil, will dwindle and perish, and the population be given up to the unmitigated consequences of a famine of the Divine ordinances."

" A subscription has therefore been opened in furtherance of the object stated in this appeal. Henry Hoare, Esq., Banker, of Fleet Street, is treasurer of the fund, the proceeds of which will be vested in government securities till the same shall be drawn for by the proper authorities in the Diocese of Ohio."

The evidence of the special object for which this fund was raised, is found in Bishop Chase's "*Plea for the West.*" He says, p. 4 : " No sooner was this appeal made to them (the English), than they met and answered it with a liberal hand. 'Take,' said they, 'our proportion in full to accomplish your great and benevolent design; but in so doing, our wishes are appropriate and just, *that what we give be regarded as a fund to be laid out in lands, or otherwise, for the permanent benefit of this and future generations.*' "

The result will show that those wishes have been strictly complied with. The money was first laid out in land, and was so kept till, in the judgment of the Trustees, it would be " otherwise " more productive. Now the land has been sold, and the fund entire invested mainly in bond and mortgage.

Subscriptions to the Ohio Theological Seminary.

The Right Rev. the Lord Bishop of London.	£20	
The Right Rev. the Lord Bishop of Durham	100	
The Right Rev. the Lord Bishop of St. David's	10	10
The Right Rev. the Lord Bishop of Chester	20	
The Right Rev. the Lord Bishop of Litchfield and Coventry	10	
Right. Hon. Lord Kenyon	50	
Right Hon. Lord Calthorpe	10	
Right Hon. Lord Barham	5	
Right Hon. Admiral Lord Gambier	20	
Right Hon. Lord Bexley	50	
Right Hon. Dowager Countess of Rosse	400	
Very Rev. the Dean of Canterbury	5	
Very Rev. the Dean of Salisbury	5	
Hon. Mr. Justice Park	10	

	£	
Adnut, Rev. T., Rector of Harlston	1	
Anonymous, Yorkshire	5	
Anonymous, by Messrs. Hoare	2	
Arnold, J. A. Esq., Lutterworth	1	1
Arnold, Miss, "	1	1
Arnold, Miss A. "	1	1
Babington, T. Esq., Rothley Temple	5	
Baldock, Mr. W., Clapham	1	
Bean, Rev. J., British Museum	5	
Bevan, S. Esq., Fosbury	5	
Belgrave, Rev. T., Rector of Kilworth	2	2
Bevan, Rev. F., Carlton Road	5	
Bickersteth, Rev. E., Islington	10	
Blackburn, Mr. P., Clapham	1	
Bolland, Rev. W.	1	
Bower, Mrs., Lutterworth	10	
Budd, Rev. Henry, Bridewell	8	
Burney, Rev. Dr., Greenwich	10	10
Buszard, M., Esq., Lutterworth	2	
Butterworth, J., Esq., M. P., Bedford Square	10	10
Butterworth, J. H., Esq., Fleet Street	2	
Carr, Rev. J. E., by Jones & Co	5	
Caton, Mr. P.	1	
Chambers, Rev. W. Rugby	2	
Chapman, Miss, by Messrs. Hoare	2	
Cholmely, Sir Montague, Bart, M. P.	10	
Cholmely, Miss S.	5	
Cleaver, Rev. W., by Messrs. Hoare	5	
Cleaver, Rev. H	5	
Clergyman, by Rev. Josiah Pratt	10	
Cobb, Rev. W. F., Nettlestead	1	
Cobb, Mrs.	1	
Coffin, General	2	
Connor, Rev. Mr., Ockbrook	1	
Connington, Rev. R. and Mrs.	2	
Cotton, Joseph, Esq., Leyton	50	
Cox, Thomas, Esq., Derby	3	3
Cox, John, Esq., "	2	2
Cox, Mrs. John, "	1	1
Cox, Henry, Esq., "	2	
Cox, Mrs. R., Spondon	2	2
Crawley, G. A., Esq., Inner Temple	10	
C. S., by Messrs. Hoare	2	
Cunningham, Rev. F., M. A., Pakefield	5	5
Dabyack, Miss, by Messrs. Hoare		
Dabyack, Miss S., by Messrs. Hoare	1	
Dale, Mrs. Robert, Ashbourne	1	
Davis, W., Esq., Leytonstone	10	10
Dewe, Rev. Joseph, Breadsall	1	1
Dicey, Mrs., Sen., Claybrook	5	
Dicey, T. E., Esq., "	10	
Doyle, Rev. J. W., Stoney Stanton	2	2
Dudley, Miss	1	1
Evans, Rev. E., Rector of Shawell	1	
Ford, Rev. J., by Messrs. Hoare	5	
Forster, W. Martin, Esq., Gower Street	5	5
Friend, by Messrs. Hoare	50	
Friend, by Rev. F. Cunningham	30	
Friend, by E. Pusey, Esq	5	5
Friend, by Mrs. Stewart	2	2
Friend, from Lincolnshire	1	1

Friends, two by Messrs. Drummond.................................£	10	
Friends, three, by Messrs. Hoare...............	3	
Gambier, Rev. F., by Messrs. Hoare.......	1	1
Gaskin, Rev. G., D.D., Stoke Newington........	5	5
Gaw, Mr. W., by Messrs. Hoare.........	1	
Gell, Rev. Philip, Matlock.........	3	3
Gipps, G., Esq., M. P., York Street....	10	
Gipps, Mrs.........	10	
Gisborne, Rev. T., Prebendary of Durham...	10	
Goodacre, J., Esq., Lutterworth.......	5	
Graham, Thomas, Esq.........	2	
Graham, Miss.........	2	
Graves, Rev. R., Reddington...	1	1
Graves, Mrs., "	1	1
Green, Rev. W., Lutterworth....	2	
Gurney, Miss E., by Messrs. Hoare....	1	
Hankey, Thomas, Esq., Fenchurch Street...	3	3
Harper, H., Esq., Jr., by Pole & Co.	1	
Harris, G., Esq., Rugby.........	1	
Hatchard, Mr., Piccadilly.....	1	
Haycock, Miss, Farnham.....	2	2
Herne, Mrs., by Pole & Co.....	1	1
Hetherington, Miss, Cottesbatch...	1	
Hewitt, Hon. James, Dublin.....	2	
Hey, Rev. Samuel, Ockbrook.....	2	2
Hindman, John, Esq., Walthamstow...	10	10
Hoare, Henry, Esq., Fleet Street....	20	
Hoare, S., Esq., Jr., Hempstead.....	21	
Holroyd, Miss D., by Messrs. Hoare.....	1	1
Homer, Rev. P., Rugby...	2	
Honey, Rev. W. D., Banbury.....	2	
Honey, Mrs. and Misses.....	4	
Horne, Rev. T. Hartwell, Pentonville.....	2	
Howard, Rev. J. G., M. A., Derby.....	1	1
Hudson, W. B., Esq., Haymarket....	10	
Hurdis, Miss, by Messrs. Hoare.....	2	
Hutton, Rev. J., Sproxton.....	1	
Inglelow, Mr. and Miss.....	2	
Jowett, Rev. H., Little Dunham.....	2	2
Jowett, Miss, "	1	1
Jowett, Rev. John, Ancaster.....	5	
Jowett, Mr. Joshua, Great Queen Street.....	2	2
Keine, Mrs., Lyme...	2	
Key, Mrs.....	1	1
Kilvington, Rev. Edward, Osset.....	10	
Lady, by Messrs. Hoare.....	1	
Lacher, E. H., Esq.....	5	
Le Grice, Miss, Rugby.....	1	
Longmire, Rev. J. M., Winkfield.....	7	
MacDanbuz, Mrs.....	5	
MacDanbuz, Mrs. Ann	5	
Mainwaring, Misses.....	5	
Maitland, Miss B. F., Shinfield Park.....	2	
Malpas, C., Esq., Inner Temple.....	1	1
Marriott, Rev. R., Cottesbatch	10	
Marriott, G. W., Esq., Queen Square	5	
Marriott, Miss, Rugby.....	5	
Marshall, Mr. T., Manchester.....	1	
Matthew, Mr. G., by Messrs. Hoare.....	1	
Mettam, Rev. G., Barwell.....	1	1
Moore, C., Esq., Middle Temple.....	15	

Moore, Rev. J. H. C., Rugby	1	
Murray, C. Esq., Ockbrook	2	
Murray, Rev. J., Whitchurch	1	
Newton, W., Esq., Derby	2	2
Packe, C. W., Esq., Prestwold	1	1
Palmer, Sir C., Bart., Wanlip Hall	10	10
Palmer, Mrs. Archdale, Cheam	2	2
Pennifeather, Mr., Great George Street	2	
Piddock, Rev. J., Ashby-de-la-Zouch	1	1
Piddock, Miss	1	1
Powell, Rev. J., Vicar of Bitteswell	2	
Powley, Mrs., Osset, Yorkshire	5	
Pusey, Hon. Philip	30	
Pusey, Philip, Esq	20	
Pusey, E., Esq., by do	5	5
Pratt, Rev. Josiah, B. D., Doughty Street	10	
Preston, Rev. M. M., Walthamstow	5	
Prince, Rev. J., Magdalen	1	1
Raikes, Rev. H.	5	
Rankin, Mrs., Bristol	2	
Reynolds, J. S., Esq., Fulham	5	5
R—— N——	5	
R. N., by Messrs. Hoare	1	
Roberts, Mrs. "	2	
ogers, Rev. J. M., Bath	200	
Sanford, G., Esq., near Bristol	5	
Schoonberg, Rev. J. D., Lutterworth	1	
Scott, Mrs., by Messrs. Hoare	5	
Seeley & Son, Messrs., Fleet Street	2	2
Shepherd, Mrs., Amport, Hants	50	
Shepley, Mrs.	2	
Simpson, Rev. R., Derby	1	1
Simpson, Mrs.	1	1
Smith, Abel, Esq., M. P.	10	
Snook, Capt. S., by Messrs. Hoare	2	
Stevenson, Mrs., Hampstead oad	15	
Sterm, Mr.	50	
Stackhouse, Mrs., by Messrs. Hoare	1	
Stackhouse, Miss, " "	1	
Stow, Mr., Greenwich	5	
Stow, Mrs.	2	
Stow, Miss	2	
Stuart, Mrs. J., by Messrs. Hoare	2	
Stratton, G. F., Esq., Upper Worton	5	
Taylor, James, Esq.	5	
Tucker, Rev. J., West Malling	5	
Turner, S. Esq., by Messrs. Hoare	5	5
Twigge, Mrs. Martha, Derby	5	
Upjohn, Capt., by Messrs. Hatchard	2	
Unwin, Rev. Edward, Derby	10	
Vansittart, Miss, Great George Street	20	
Ward, Rev. Edward, Iver, Bucks	5	
Ward, Rev. Edward's pupils	2	
Watkins, Rev. H. G., M. A.	2	2
Wawn, Rev. J. D., Stanton	1	1
Wayland, J. Esq., Jr.	5	
Wilberforce, W., Esq., M. P.	10	
Widow's Mite, from an American	1	
Woodall, Rev. W., Rector of Bramstone	1	1
Woodroffe, Rev. T., by Messrs. Hoare	1	1
Wool, Rev. Dr., Head Master Rugby	10	
Sums under 20s	4	7

SUBSCRIPTIONS CONTINUED.

ASHBOURNE.

	£	s.	d.
By ———— ————	£ 6	9	

BRADFORD, YORKSHIRE.

By Mr. John Rand.	15	16	

CARLISLE.
By Rev. John Fawcet.

Bowes, Mrs	1	1
Dixon, John, Esq	2	2
Fawcet, Rev. John, M. A.	2	2
Ferguson, Mrs. G	2	2
Friend	3	3
Friend	3	3
Friends, several	5	5
Graham, J. H., Esq	2	2
Hollingsworth, G. L., Esq	1	1
Lodge, Mrs	2	2

HALIFAX:
By Rev. S. Knight.

	90	10

HULL.
By Rev. John Scott.

Alder, G., Esq	5	5
Atkinson, A., Esq	1	1
Beverly Grammar School boys	1	19
Bodley, W. H., Esq., M. D.	1	1
Bodley, Mrs	1	1
Carrick, J., Esq	1	
Cartwright, Miss R.	1	
Dickinson, S., Esq	5	5
Dikes, Rev. T., LL. B	2	2
Dikes, Mr. T	1	1
Dikes, Mr. W.	1	1
Eyre, Rev. Mr	1	1
Friend	1	1
Frost, Chas., Esq	1	1
Frost, Mrs. J.	1	1
Gleadow, R., Esq	1	1
Grainger, Rev. L	1	
" for a friend	5	5
Green, Mrs	2	
Hall, Mrs	1	
Hildyard, Rev. W., M. A	1	1
Horner, S., Esq., Jr	1	1
Horner, S., Esq	1	1
Howard, Mrs. A	10	10
" " for a friend	10	10
Hudson, Mr. J	1	1
Hustwick, Mr. R	1	1
Jarrett, W., Esq	1	1
King, Mr. S.	1	1
King, Mr. R.,	1	1
Knight, Rev. W., B. A.	1	1
Lawrence, Mrs	1	
Lowthrop, Mr	1	
Lutwidge, C., Esq	1	1
Martin, S., Esq	1	
Moxon, W., Esq	1	

Norman, Miss	£ 1	
Rennard, Mrs.	5	5
" " for Mrs. Jewett.	5	5
Richards, Rev. Mr	1	1
Richmond, Miss	5	5
Roberts, Rev. J. H.	1	
Robinson, Mr. T	1	11
Sandwith, Mrs	1	
Scott, Rev. J., M. A	1	1
Sykes, Mrs. J	5	5
Teale, Mrs	1	1
Terry, Addison, Esq	5	5
Thompson, Misses	1	
Thornton, J., Esq	1	1
Todd, J., Esq	1	
Turnbull, A., Esq., M. D	1	
Turner, Mrs., Ferridy	2	
Watson, J. K., Esq.,	5	
Watson, Mrs. J. K	1	1
Wells, Mr. W	1	1
Westoby, E., Esq	1	1
Wilson, Mr. J	1	1
Sums under 20s	6	6

LEEDS.
By T. S. B. Reade, Esq.

Armitage, Miss	2	
Blayds, Mrs	4	
Blayds, Miss		
Blayds, John, Esq., Jr	3	
Blayds, Mrs. John	1	
Browne, Mrs	5	
Browne, Miss E	1	1
Fawcet, Joseph, Esq	1	
Fenton & Sadler, Messrs	7	
Friend	1	1
Friend	1	
Friend to the cause	2	2
Friend, for Rev. Mr. Holme	3	5
Hargrave, Mrs	1	
Hey, W., Esq	5	
Hey, Mr. W., Jr	2	
Holdroyd, Mrs	1	
Kirshener, Mrs	2	
Reade, T. S. B., Esq	5	
Rhodes, Miss C	1	1
Robinson, Miss C	1	1
Walker, Rev. G	2	
Wilk, W., Esq	3	
Sums under 20s	1	

LIVERPOOL.
By Rev. Ambrose Dawson.

Aspinall, Mrs. T	5	
Aspinall, Mr. W	1	1
Aspinall, Miss E	1	1
Bickersteth, Mrs	1	1
Bird, Miss	1	

Name	£	
Blake, Mr. G	£1	
Bowsted, Rev. T. S., M. A	1	
Buddicom, Rev. R. P., M. A	1	1
Crosthwaite, Mr	5	
Crosthwaite, Mr. J	1	1
Dawson, Rev. A., B. D	5	
Driffield, Rev. G	1	1
Eden, J., Esq	1	1
Jones, Rev. J., M. A	1	1
Knowles, Mr. J	1	1
Mollyneaux, Mrs. A	2	
Raffles, Rev. Dr	1	1
Robinson, Messrs. G. & J.	1	1
Small sums	1	2
Sums under 20s	3	3

MANCHESTER.
By Timothy Wiggin, Esq.

Name	£	
Allen, Mr	1	
Ashton & Co., Messrs	5	
Ayrton, Mr. J	1	
Barge & Co., Messrs	3	
Barrow, Miss	2	
Barton, J., Esq	5	
Bateman, Mrs	2	2
Bateman, Mrs. T., Jr	1	1
Baxter, Mr. E	2	
Beaver, Hugh, Esq	5	
Bentley & Wilkinson, Messrs	3	
Birch, Mrs	1	
Blackwall, Mr. T	3	
Booth, Rev. S., M. A	5	
Bradley, Mr. B	1	1
Bridge, Mr	1	
Brierly, J., Esq	5	
Brooks, S. R., Esq	5	
Brooks, Mr. S.	2	2
Burgess, Mr. J	1	
Burgess, Mr. A	1	
Burton, Mr. J	1	
Butterworth & Brooks	5	
Byron, Mrs	5	
Calvert, Very Rev. T. D. D., Ward of Manchester	5	
Cardwell, Mr. T	3	
Chase, B. W., Esq	10	
Chesshyre, Mrs	2	
Chesshyre, Miss	1	
Chippendall, J., Esq	5	
Clegg, widow and sons	4	4
Clogg, Mr. R.	3	
Davies, Mr. R	1	
Dickinson, Mrs	5	
Dixon, Mr. F	1	
Douglass, Miss	2	
Duckworth, Mr. W	1	
Elsdale, Rev. R.	2	10
Ethelston, Rev. C. W	3	
Ferrier, Miss	2	
Fletcher, S., Esq	5	
Fort, Brothers & Co., Messrs	2	2

Name	£	
Forths & Co, Messrs	£1	
Fraser, Mr. J. W	1	1
Friend, by Miss C. Wiggins	5	
Friend to Education	5	
Friend	4	4
Friends, three	3	
Gardner, Mr	2	2
Grant, D., Esq	5	
Grundy & Bearclock	3	
Hadfield, G., Esq	5	
Haigh, Brothers, & Charles	5	
Harbottle, Mr. T	1	
Hardy, Mrs	1	
Harrison & Sons, Messrs	3	
Heywood, Mr. R	3	
Hitchin, Jonathan, Esq	5	
Hollist, Rev. J	1	1
Horne, Miss	1	
Horridge & Holmes, Messrs	5	5
Holme, Mr. D	2	
Ingham, Mr	1	
Jones, Mr. J. S	2	
Kay, J., Esq	5	
Kennedy, J., Esq	5	
Leese, Mr.	1	
Lomas, Mr. W	1	
Lowe & Co., Messrs	5	
Loyd, E., Esq	5	
Lyon, Mr. J	1	
Macfarline, Mr. J	2	2
Marris, Mr. F	2	
Marshall, Mrs	2	
Norris, J, Esq	1	
Norris, Mr. E	2	
Oughton, Mr. J	1	1
Parker, Messrs. T & R	5	5
Piccope, Rev. J	1	1
Randall, Rev. M	1	
Remington, Rev. R	1	1
Robinson, Mr. W	2	
Scarr, Petty & Swain	5	
Scarr, Mr. R	2	2
Sharp, Mr. T	3	
Shaw, Rev. E. B	1	
Slacks, Miss	2	2
Smith, Rev. J., D. D	3	
Smith, Mr. R	2	
Smith, Mr	1	
Stocks, S. Esq	5	
Stocks, Mr. S., Jr	2	2
Todd, J., Esq	10	
Townend, Mr. W	2	2
Townend, Mr. T	1	
Towner, Mr. E. W.	5	
Turner, Mr. W	3	
Tweddell, Rev. R	2	
Vaudray, Mr. J	1	
Walker, Mr. J	2	
Walton, Mr. J	1	
Walton, Mr. J	1	
Walkins, T. Esq	5	

Name	£	s
Whitworth, Mr. A	£1	
Wiggin, T., Esq	70	
Wiggin, Mrs	10	
Wiggin, Mr. B. H	10	
Wiggin, Miss	5	
Wiggin, Miss C	5	
Williams, Mr. W	2	
Williams, Mrs	1	
Wilson, Mr. W. J	1	
Wood & Sons, Messrs	3	3
Wood & Westhead, Messrs	2	
Worseley, T. C., Esq	5	5
Worthington, T., Esq	5	
Wray, Rev. C. D	2	
Wright, ——, Esq	5	
Wright, Mrs	1	
Wyatt, Mr	1	
Sums under 20s		10

NOTTINGHAM.
By the Rev. J. B. Stuart.

Name	£	s
Almond, Rev. R. W., A. M	1	1
Anderson, Rev. E., B D	1	
Barnet, Mr. C	1	1
Bird, Rev. Mr	1	1
Bolton, T., Esq	5	
Brocksop, Mrs	1	
Browne, Ven. Archdeacon	3	
Clarke, Mr. C. H	2	2
Cocher, Mrs	1	
Davys, Rev. Owen	1	
Davys, Miss	1	
Elliott, Mrs	3	
Friend	1	
Greaves, E., Esq	1	1
Hazard, Mr	2	
Holdsworth, Miss	2	
Howard, Rev. Wm	1	1
Jeffs, Miss	1	
Maddock, Rev. B., and friends,	2	2
Maddock, Mr	2	
Middlemore, Mrs	1	
Norris, Mrs	3	
Nixon, Mr	1	
Rolleston, Rev. J., M. A	1	1
Smith, Henry, Esq	5	
Stones, Mr	1	1
Storer, Dr	2	2
Storer, Rev. John, M. A	2	
Stuart, Rev. J. B., M. A	3	
Sykes, Mr. R. L	1	1
Taylor, Mrs	1	1
Towle, Mr	1	
Trentham, Mr	2	2
W. II., Mrs	1	
Wildsmith, Mr	1	1
Wright, John S., Esq	5	
Sums under 20s	24	19

YORK.
By W. Gray, Esq.

Name	£	s
Acaster, Rev. J	5	
Anonymous, by Rev. W. Gray	£5	
Anonymous	1	1
Anonymous	1	
Belwood, Mrs	1	
Benson, Mrs	10	
Blanchard, Mrs., collected am'g Sabbath-school visitors	9	
Bowman, Miss	1	1
Brown, Mrs	1	1
Brown, Mr. G	1	
Calvert, Mrs	1	
Camidge, Mr	1	
Cheap, Rev. A., *Knaresborough*,	1	1
Cooplang, Rev. G	1	1
Dallin, Rev. James	50	
Darnell, Miss	1	
Dodsworth, Mrs	2	2
Ewbank, Mrs. J	5	
Forrest, Rev. R	2	2
Frank, Miss	5	
Fretwell, Mrs	1	1
Friend to Missions	1	1
Friends, two, "	1	
Gimber, Mrs	5	
Graham, Rev. J	2	
Gray, W., Esq	10	
Gray, Mrs	5	
Gray, Mr. Jonathan	3	3
Gray, Rev. Edmund	2	2
Grayson, Rev. Isaac	1	1
Harvey, Mrs	5	
Hinks, Mr	2	2
Jennings, T., Esq	1	1
Lawton, Mr	1	1
Lawton, Mrs	1	1
Moore, Miss	1	
Moore, Miss F	1	
Morris, Miss	1	1
Overton, Rev. J	2	2
Percival, Misses	1	1
Prest, Mrs	5	
Price, Thomas, Esq	2	2
Price, Mrs	1	
Richardson, Mrs	3	
Richardson, Rev. James	2	2
Richardson, Rev. T	1	1
Robinson, Miss	1	1
Russell, David, Esq	5	
Russell, Rev. W. B	2	
Russell, Mr. James	1	1
Russell, Mrs. James	1	1
Smith, Miss	2	2
Stillingfleet, Rev. E. W	1	
Thompson, Mrs	10	
Thompson, Mr. W	1	1
Thompson, Mrs. W	1	1
Thorpe, Anthony, Esq	5	
Thorpe, Mrs	2	
Thorpe, Mr. G., *Kirton*	1	1
Willey, Jocelyn, Esq	5	
Whytehead, Mrs	1	1
Sums under 20s	1	16

It is supposed that the sum of £100, given by Lady Rosse for the specific purpose of aiding in the erection of a College Chapel, is included in the £400 credited to her in the above list. Possibly, it is not. At any rate, the commemoration of this gift, by naming the building after her—Rosse Chapel—was no more than a just tribute to her Christian generosity. She gave, at the same time, another £100 to aid the weak parishes of that day in building churches.

Thus far is the account published by the London Trustees, May 22, 1824. It is not to be understood, however, as being the account rendered upon their final settlement with Bishop Chase, as it is less than half the amount collected in England. The full account can not be found in this country. Should any friend in England fall in with it, he will confer a favor by indicating where, and how, it may be obtained, that the names of all the donors may be remembered. This loss makes Bishop Chase's accounts none the less satisfactory, as his statement, often published in this country, that the whole amount was rising $30,000 was approved, at least by the silence of the English Trustees.

The names, however, of several of the other donors, will appear from the following extracts from Bishop Chase's correspondence and addresses, after his return to this country:

"When Bishop Chase arrived in England, a train of providences prepared the way for his favorable reception, and the interesting claims of religion and learning, in Ohio, were taken hold of by men who stand highest among the examples of Christian benevolence in England. Among these were Lords Gambier, Kenyon, and Bexley, and Sir Thomas Acland, among the nobility, and Dr. Gaskin, Mr. Pratt, Mr. Marriott, and others, some of the most distinguished of the clergy and gentry. An appeal, addressed to the British public, was prepared by the editors of the *Christian Observer*, and *Christian Guardian*, by several of the officers of the Society for Promoting Christian Knowledge, and of the Church Missionary Society; an appeal which eventuated in raising at least $30,000."—*Committee of the Ohio Convention.*

Most interesting letters (the originals of which, neatly bound in a volume, have lately been presented to the library of the Institution by Rev. Dudley Chase) were addressed to Bishop Chase, from a daughter of the celebrated Jones, of Nayland, Admiral Lord

Gambier, Lord Kenyon, the Bishop of London, the Archbishop of Canterbury, and Lord Bexley.

The following is from the daughter of a highly respectable clergyman. At the time this was written she was only fourteen years of age, and so great was her interest, that by her industry she had raised nearly $35 toward the object, and says to Bishop Chase: "May I beg of you to give my affectionate love to your children, and tell them how little deserving I feel myself of their love, and of my most honorable title of Mary Ohio. I wish it were in my power to prove myself better entitled to one and the other; but I believe I shall easily gain credence when I say, that to repay to Ohio one iota of those blessings which I have received from her, would be a real happiness to me. * * I will thank you for your great kindness to me, who can only wish you well, and can plead your cause in no other way than by sometimes whispering, 'there is a rose in the West, whose head is drooping for want of watering, and her stem bending for want of propping.'"

One of the contributors that should by no means be forgotten, was Mrs. Hannah More, who took a deep interest in Bishop Chase's plans, and herself subscribed £50.

Bishop Chase, in his address to the Convention in 1824, says of the English people, in reference to the Ohio Seminary: " Never was benevolence more disinterested; never was zeal more active. The task of solicitation being assumed by the most respectable characters, the rich feasts of intellectual intercourse and Christian courteousness were every-where spread before me."

One occurrence, or rather series of occurrences, seems stranger than fiction. One day, long before Bishop Chase thought of ever going to England, having been at work on his farm at Worthington, at the close of the day he penned a letter to Dr. Jarvis, in answer to one of inquiry respecting the condition of the Church in the West. This letter became a little stained with blood from a crack in the Bishop's hand, for which he apologized, by saying he had just come in from work. Dr. Jarvis, in answer to inquiries from one of the Scottish Bishops respecting the condition of the Church in this country, sent Bishop Chase's letter just as he had received it. The daughter of this Bishop (Duff. McFarlane) was then in England, at the death-bed of John Bowdler, Esq., when she received a letter from her father, inclosing that sent by Dr. Jarvis, from Bishop Chase. She read the letter to the dying man, and was directed by him to take from his drawer a purse containing ten guineas, and by the first convenient opportunity send it to Bishop Chase. When in after years Bishop Chase was in England, Duff. McFarlane invited him to breakfast one morning, after which she astonished him by showing him his own letter to Dr. Jarvis, and handing over the ten guineas.

Bishop Chase, being on an agency for the Church, refused to receive any private gifts, and appropriated it for the purchase of communion plate for Rosse Chapel, which was afterward consumed in Bishop Chase's house in Michigan.

By the contributions of some friends a set of plate for the administration of the communion in private was also purchased for the use of the *Bishop of Ohio*.

In 1825, Bishop C. says : " with respect to our affairs in England, it becomes my duty to state that, besides the *permanent* fund, now rising five thousand guineas, there remained, at the last advices, a large collection of books still in London, given by different most benevolent individuals; also, the stereotype plates for our Prayer-Book, and a separate fund for a most complete set of printing types, to carry into effect an essential part of our plan. Of the books given in England, already arrived in America, some, together with 112 pairs of blankets, a large pair of globes (given by Miss Ann Rust), and a set of mathematical instruments, are on the way from New York hither.

In 1826, mention is made in Bishop Chase's address as follows : " It will be remembered that this complete and ample set of type, together with £100 sterling, to purchase a printing press in this country, is the avails of a most munificent subscription, separate from that of the fund, which subscription was originated and circulated among the ladies of the nobility of England by that most excellent person, Lady Acland, of Devonshire. * * I am happy to add that, by a letter received yesterday from my worthy and most esteemed friend, G. W. Marriott, Esq., of London, it appears that this fountain of benevolence is not yet dried up. In his letter dated March 5th, he observes, 'there is a surplus of £50 from the printing press subscription. This Sir Thomas Acland begs me to dispose of.' "

Intelligence had also been received that an organ for the chapel had been completed, and five hundred and forty-six volumes added to the library.

In 1827, it is further stated: "In England, too, the fountain is by no means exhausted. A box of books, worth several hundred dollars — including Walton's Polyglot Bible, and many of the Fathers and standard books—was sent us during the last winter, as the gift of the Right Hon. Lord Kenyon and the Rev. Dr. Ward, of Great Horenly; and I am lately informed that Mrs. Walker, daughter of the late excellent William Jones, of Nayland, has caused to be prepared, in London, a most valuable telescope for the use of the students of Kenyon College."

In 1830, appears Bishop Chase's final notice of the English benefactions, as follows: "A plain statement of facts which have taken place since the Rev. Mr. West went to England, if I recollect aright, is this: I received from Lord Kenyon, to be considered as the legacy of his daughter, the late Hon. Margaret Langham, £500; also, in a draft from Thomas Bates, Esq., £100; also, from G. W. Marriott, Esq., of London, as the avails of Mr. West's collection, £400—making in all £1,000."

Such are the pleasing evidences of the kind interest which the English Church took in the founding of the Theological Seminary of the Diocese of Ohio, and Kenyon College.

EFFORTS MADE FOR THE SEMINARY AND COLLEGE IN THE UNITED STATES, BY BISHOP CHASE.

It will be proper next, to consider the efforts made by Bishop Chase, in behalf of these institutions, in his own country. His first step, after returning from England, was to fix upon a site for the Seminary and College. His conditional deed of donation left him at liberty to seek another location, if Henry Clay should approve. Mrs. Betsey Reed, of Putnam, O., had made a liberal offer of 1,000 acres of land on Elm Creek, twelve miles north of Columbus. This was first adopted, and something was done toward a beginning upon it.

Meanwhile Bishop Chase had his attention called, by Daniel S. Norton, Esq., and Henry B. Curtis, Esq., of Mount Vernon, to a tract of land, 8,000 acres, in Knox county, lying five miles east of the county-seat. The land was owned by William Hogg, Esq., of Brownsville, Penn., and appeared to Bishop C. so well adapted to his purpose, that he immediately made a contract for it at $3 per acre, subject to the approval of the Trustees and Henry Clay. After mature deliberation, it was decided to approve the purchase, and locate the Seminary where it now is. Mr. Hogg generously consented to donate one-fourth of the price of the land, $6,000, and upon the receipt of $18,000, conveyed the title to the Trustees of the Theological Seminary of the Diocese of Ohio. Then commenced the struggles which have resulted in the establishment of the present institutions—the Theological Seminary of the Diocese of Ohio, and Kenyon College.

The following is an extract from an "*Appeal in behalf of Religion and Learning in Ohio,*" published by Bishop Chase, and dated Nov. 21, 1826. After noticing the results of his appeal to English friends, he says:

"With a heart deeply penetrated by grateful emotions for such unexampled benevolence from a *foreign* fountain, the undersigned would turn with reasonable confidence, and with great respect, to his own countrymen; and while he does so, he offers an anxious prayer to God, that he may find favor in their sight.

"He earnestly desires them to consider, that the steps taken by the undersigned have been approved by the Christian world, and by his own community in Ohio in particular; that the Convention of Ohio having framed a constitution, and appointed trustees of the intended institution in conformity to acknowledged principles, the civil legislature has established the same as a corporate body; that a tract of land of great intrinsic worth, especially as a future sure and increasing revenue to the College, has been purchased at a very reduced price, and the Seminary and College permanently fixed thereon; and that for the payment of this land, consisting of 8,000 acres, the funds collected in England have, in a good measure, been pledged.

"The result of all this is *the imperious necessity of obtaining means to erect the requisite buildings.* That this necessity may appear undisputed, let the greatness of the undertaking, and the smallness of the means hitherto obtained, (however munificent in themselves,) be compared, and how conspicuous will be the disparity! What college was ever reared with only $30,000? If **we** saw our building *now* erected, and if the funds obtained in England were *now* at interest, the whole would constitute but a *beginning*—but the foundation of so great a work. What, then, must be the solicitude of every true Christian and lover of his country, for the fate of this benevolent work, when he is told that the buildings are scarcely *commenced*, and the funds, according to the designs of the donors, are invested more for *permanent* than for *present* use? Was it unreasonable, when the undersigned stipulated with the benefactors in England, that if they would contribute toward the *permanent* fund, his own country, *America*, would furnish means for the buildings? To refuse such a condition, would have been a stain on his native land. The honor, therefore, of the American name, unites with the goodness of the cause, in sustaining the fervent hope and humble trust that this stipulation will be fulfilled. The Ohio Seminary will succeed. Americans will do something to erect the buildings, when their religious brethren in England have done so much for its permanent support.   *   *   *   * God save our country from ignorance and sin, through Jesus Christ our Lord.   PHILANDER CHASE."

"P. S. Such benevolent persons as find it in their hearts to contribute, are requested to send their benefactions to either of the following gentlemen :

> Leonard Kip, Esq., *President of the North River Bank.*
> William Jones, Esq., *Philadelphia.*
> Com. Tingey, *Washington.*
> Joseph McNeil, Esq., *New Orleans.*
> Charles Sigourney, Esq., *Hartford.*
> E. A. Newton, Esq., *Boston.*"

To the above appeal there was, as will hereafter appear, a generous response.

This *plea* was made in 1826. In 1828, we find Bishop Chase entreating Congress for a grant of a township of land. In this he was disappointed. A bill passed the Senate, but in the House was crowded out by a press of business. Though foiled in this, he did not despair. In trying times Bishop Chase was never without an expedient. When there was no opposition nor difficulty, he might be at a loss what to do, and how to expend his mighty energies; but when wind and current were against him, he commonly found in them the very elements of success.

At this time he published his "*Star in the West; or, Kenyon College in the Year of our Lord*, 1828."

After giving a history of his application to Congress and its failure, and recounting the pressing necessities of the College, Bishop Chase says: *A small sum only is asked of every friend of every name and class.* * * Whoever reads this is, therefore, most respectfully and earnestly entreated to send ONE DOLLAR in aid of the present struggles of Kenyon College." What the precise effect of this plea was, it is impossible now to say. It is said that the dollars came to Gambier as leaves fall in Autumn, but there is no distinction made in the account rendered, between the results of this and of the former *appeal*.

In the year 1829, Bishop Chase rendered the following account of all the donations he had received in this country; and as at the close he appeals to the donors themselves, to inform him if any thing was omitted, and then published it to the world, it affords the best evidence the case admits of, that all the funds contributed were accounted for:

SUBSCRIBERS TO KENYON COLLEGE IN OHIO.

	Cash.	Produce.	Labor.
Armstrong, Gabriel	$5 00		
Backus, Miss, *Chillicothe*	5 00		
Banning, Anthony		$220 00	
Barber, Josiah	5 00		
Barber, Sophia	5 00		
Barr, John		5 00	
Beall, R.	25 00		
Beckwith, E. & A.		5 00	
Benedict, Platt		1 00	
Bevans, M. & G.		10 00	
Bevans, William		6 50	
Bird, Sylvanus		3 00	
Bird, Elisha		1 00	
Bowman, S.	10 00		
Bronson, Thomas G.		10 00	
Bronson, C. P.		10 00	
Bronson, Rebecca		5 00	
Brown, R. M.		12 00	
Bryant, Gilman		50 00	
Burr, J. N., Dr.		10 00	
Burr, Timothy Dr.		100 00	
Carter, James		2 00	
Cash, *Marietta*	1 00		
Case, Farren	10 00		
Cass, Jonathan	10 00		
Chapman, Geo.	3 00		
Chittenden, M.	1 00		
Christmas, John	25 00		
Clark, John	10 00		

SUBSCRIBERS TO KENYON COLLEGE IN OHIO—CONTINUED.

	Cash.	Produce.	Labor.
Coen, William		$25 00	
Converse, D.	$6 00	24 00	
Cox, L.	5 00		
Cunningham, Alexander.	5 00		
Cunningham, William	5 00		
Cunningham, John.	5 00		
Cunningham, James	5 00		
Curtis, Henry B.		46 00	
Curtis, Hosmer			$7 25
Chillicothe, several persons who paid the debt due by Seminary to John Elliott	13 10		
Darling, Abraham			10 00
Davidson, John E.		10 00	
Dunlevy, Daniel.	10 00		
Davis, Thomas	25 00		
Dickenson, W. R.		75 00	
Davis, Thomas T.			10 00
Dugan, James.	8 00		
Delano, A.	1 00		
Edwards, Edmund			5 00
Elliott, Hugh.		20 00	
Elliott, Andrew		5 00	
Elliott, Charles, jun.		1 60	
Elliott, James.			12 50
Elliott, Charles, *Knox county*	1 00	80 00	
Elliott, Alexander		50 00	
Elliott, Simon.	2 00		
Ewalt, J., jun.			5 00
Evarts, Milo	1 00		
Farquhar, W. Y.	7 60	2 40	
Fuller, Nathaniel.	10 00		
Gambier, Post Office	1 12		
Griffin, Apollos		10 00	
Glasgow, John.	5 00		
Goddard, Charles B.	1 00		
Gibbs, Elisha, 2,000 shingles.		4 00	
Hadley, Isaac			10 00
Hammel, John			10 00
Hawn, John, jun.		43 50	
Hedges, Elzey.	5 00		
Henderson, John	2 00		
Henderson, Robert	3 00		
Henry, S. S.	10 00		
Hickox, John	6 00		
Higgins, Joseph.			2 00
Hogg, George.	90 00		
Houck, Jacob.	4 50		
House, Richard	15 00		
Huddle, Joseph.	5 00		
Humphrey, Chauncey.		20 00	
Humphrey, *Burton*	1 00		
Irvine, James.	5 00		
Jones, Mrs., *Chillicothe*	2 00		
Jennings, Joseph.	1 50		
Johnson, I. D.		5 00	
Johnston, Rev. Samuel	8 00		
King, John G.	5 00		
King, Mrs. Edward.	1 00		

SUBSCRIBERS TO KENYON COLLEGE IN OHIO—CONTINUED.

	IN WHAT PAID.		
	Cash.	Produce.	Labor.
Lane, E.	$6 00		
Lemort, Laban	25 00		
Lewis, Edward	2 00		
Lamson, W. K.	4 00		
Martin, Jacob			$20 00
Martin, James		$22 35	7 45
McCadden, John	15 00		
McCurdy, Richard L.	10 00		
McGibeny, James		22 00	
Maxwell, Robert (by J. Dugan)	2 00		
Maxwell, Robert	1 00		
Maxwell, Thomas	5 00		
Melick, Jonas		12 50	
Melick, George		50 00	20 00
Mefford, William		15 00	
Miller, Eli		50 00	
Miller, Ira	5 00		
Monroe, Joseph F.		25 00	
Monson, Harmer	1 00		
Morehead, William	4 00		
Morton, David			4 30
Morse, Rev. Intrepid	100 00		
Mott, Samuel		32 75	
Murray, Adam		8 00	
Morgan, Jane	1 00		
Nettleton, Dr. C.			25 00
Norton, D. S.		500 00	
Norton, P. L.		50 00	
Nye, Arius	10 00		
" second gift	2 50		
Parker, J.	10 00		
Parker, Cyrus	1 00		
Pigman, John H.			10 00
Plummer, Philip	10 00		
Prichard, A. P.		5 00	
Prince, J. & D.	20 00	30 00	
Purdy, James	5 00		
Pyle, Adam	10 00		
Renfrew, James	5 00		
Rogers, J. B.		50 00	
Rogers, Timothy W.		10 00	
Ruggles, Benjamin	10 00		
Sapp, W. R.			15 00
Sawyer, John			25 00
Sergeant, B. B.	5 00		
Shaw, John			50 00
Shepherd, *Huron county*	5 00		
Sheffield, George	5 00		
Shelton, Selah			10 00
Sibley, Nancy		5 00	
Sibley, Stephen		5 00	
Smith, William		25 00	
Sparrow, Samuel		50 00	
Stephenson, John		4 80	
Stevenson, D. D.			5 00
Stibbs, J.	25 00		
Stone, Catherine	1 50		
Stone, Mary	1 00		

SUBSCRIBERS TO KENYON COLLEGE IN OHIO—CONTINUED.

	IN WHAT PAID.		
	Cash.	Produce.	Labor.
Terry, Warner...			$15 73
Terry, Emily	$10 00		
Thompson, Robert C.	5 00		
Trimble, John..		$22 75	27 25
Turner, William..		5 00	
Ward, Jonas		10 00	
Warden, J. W...		30 00	21 51
Warner, Justus...		5 00	
Warner, Clarissa.......................................		5 00	
Warner, James..		12 00	
Wells, Bazaleel		100 00	
Wells, Franklin..		5 00	
Welton, Ebenezer		5 0J	
Wheaton, Elmas..	5 00		
Willard, G. V.	5 00		
Willard, Gustavus..........	1 00		
Wilson, Robert...		60 00	
Woodbridge, Dudley..................................	100 L0		
Woodward, Amos..		12 00	
Woodward, Gordon	5 00		
Woodbridge, Chillicothe	1 00		
Zimmerman, G..		25 00	

The following articles have also been received for the use of the Seminary:

From Mrs. Little and Mrs. Lamb, *Delaware*, 30 yards cotton sheeting.
From Rev. I. Morse, *Steubenville*, 12 yards bed ticking.
From Mrs. Turner, *Canfield*, 1 pair sheets, and 1 pair pillow cases.
From Mrs. S. Bradley, *Canfield*, 1 sheet and 1 pair pillow cases.
From Mrs. Ruggles, 1 sheet and 1 pair pillow cases.
From ———, 1 sheet and 1 pair pillow cases, marked S. S.
From P. Basset, tow cloth for bed.
From   "   "   1 towel.

N. B. For the sake of brevity we have placed under produce all subscriptions received, which have not been paid in cash or labor.

SUBSCRIBERS TO KENYON COLLEGE IN THE UNITED STATES, EXCLUSIVE OF OHIO.

Anonymous (Doubloon), Philadelphia.................$ 16	Adams, Seth, Jr., Providence, R. I.........................$ 5
Ashurst, Richard 50	Ashley, Mr. and Mrs., Newburyport........................ 5
Anonymous, by Mrs. Juliana Miller, Philadelphia. 24	A. B., by Mr. Newton......... 10
Allen, Thomas N., Philadel'a 5	Andrews, Henry................. 5
Andrews, J., " 5	Adams, J. Q., President U. S. 100
Anderson, Nicholas, New York 10	Atkinson's partner............... 5
Allen, Jeremiah, Providence, R. I........................ 25	Anonymous, Rochester......... 1
Allen, Candice, Providence, R. I...................... 20	Anderson, G., Hagarstown, Md. 1
Allen, Philip, Providence, R. I. 5	Anonymous, Portsmouth,...... 3
Allen, Crawford, Providence, R. I........................ 10	Anonymous, Newbury, C. H... 6
	Ashurst, Philadelphia........... 50
	Beatty, John, Philadelphia... 10

Basden, John Robert, Phila. $	1	
Brinton, J. H. " ...	50	
Burd, Edward, " ...	50	
Blackwell, Rev. Dr. " ...	20	
Brook, Mrs. " ..	2	
Bodey, Mrs. " ...	1 50	
Barry, Mrs. Com. " ...	10	
Bevan, M. L. " ...	5	
Brown, Lawrence, " ...	5	
Blight, George, " ...	20	
Brincle, Rev. S. C. "	5	
Burtus, James A., New York.	50	
Babcock, B. T. "	20	
Burtus, Mrs. J. A. "	10	
Brook, Thomas, "	10	
Baker, C. "	25	
Butcher, Samuel, "	10	
Boggs, James, "	20	
Burk, John, "	4	
Baldwin & Forest, "	10	
Blodget, Wm. Providence, R.I.	25	
Blodget, Samuel, "	20	
Bradley, Miss, "	3	
Babcock, Mr., Boston...	20	
Brimmer, Mrs. "	15	
Burroughs, Mr. & Mrs. "	30	
Brown and E. Upham, Misses, Portsmouth, N. H.............	7	
B., Mrs., and her sister, Newport.:...............	3	
Bartlet, Mr., Newport.........	50	
Bell, Mrs. Ann, Boston.	5	
Bell, Miss Martha, "	5	
Bell, Miss Catherine; "	5	
Boston lady, "	5	
Bigelow, Abraham, "	30	
Bangs, Mr. "	1	
Boyls, Rev. J. "	2	
Bond, W. "	5	
B., Mr. "	10	
Bever, Thomas, "	5	
Baker, Miss Mary, Georgetown, D. C......... ..	7	
Blackford, Mrs. Mary............	5	
Byles, Misses, Boston.........	2	
Beatty, Eli. Hagerstown, M. D.	1	
Brewer, Charles, Pittsburgh,	5	
Barns, Rev. A., New Jersey...	2	
"Bedford, New York,"	50	
"Be not weary in well doing," Portland, Me......:...........	1	
Barton, and E. Smith, St. Francisville, M...............	5	
Bayley, Rev. Kiah, Griesborough, Va............	1	
His friends...................	2	
Beach, Mrs. N. N., Hartford...	10	
Burgess, Mr., West Union...	1	
Bloodgood, De Witt............	25	
Bethel Church, Vt.............	8 25	
Boyd, Rev. George.............	10	
Banks, Mrs. George, N. Y...	1	

Buel, David, Troy, N. Y......	10	
Bacon, E., collected at the South, and paid on 3d July, 1827, into N. River Bank, N. Y......................	51	
Bacon, E., balance in Bank...		
Caldwell, Mrs. Ann, Philadel'a	0	
Coxe, Dr. John Redman "	50	
Clarke, Ephraim, "		
Curtis, John H.,		
Clapier, L.,		
Cash,		
Clapp, Harvey T., "	5	
Cash 1 50, cash 5, cash 5, cash 25c., cash 2, "	13 75	
Cornegys, Cornelius, "	10	
Cameron, Mrs., "	100	
Chapman, Dr., "	20	
Cash, by a lady, '	5	
College prints,	1	
Chapman, Mrs.,	5	
Cash, by a lady,	5	
Cooke, E. W.,	5	
College print, "	50	
Cash 5, 5, 3, 1, 2, 2, 2, 1 50, 2, 5, 3, "	31 50	
Cash 5, 5, 2, 50c., 3, "	15 50	
Cash, inclosed, "	2 00	
Cash by Mr. Robins, "	1	
Cash, by Mrs. M. Chase, "	5	
Campbell, C., '	5	
Coleman, William, "	20	
Coleman, James, "	20	
Cash, New York,	25	
Cash (Kellogg), "	20	
Carow, Isaac, "	50	
Cotton, Mrs. Sarah, "	15	
Cash, By C. C. M., "	10	
Chester, W. W., "	50	
Coleman, Mrs., Lancaster, P'a.	50	
Coleman, Edward, "	50	
Castor, John G., N. Y........	50	
Cash, by Rev. Mr. Grammer, Bath Parish, Dinwiddie Co., Va.	40	
Crocker, Rev. N. B., Providence, R. I............	6	
Cash, Mr. W., Providence, R. I.	10	
Cash, by Mrs. P., Boston......	5	
Coffin, Miss, "	5	
Cash, Portland, 5, 5, 2, 20c.	12 20	
C. H. T. "	2	
Collection, Newburyport,	21	
Collection, Salem,	20	
Clark, Fred. Boston.	25	
Clark, Thomas, "	5	
Clark, Sarah, "	2	
Clark, Lucy A.,	2	
Clark, H. A.,	2	
Conant, Betsey, "	2	
Collection, 2nd, at Salem,...	33	
Casnove, Charles, ...	20	

Collection in Christ Church, Boston ....$ 37 38
Coleman, Stephen, Boston,...... 5
Collection in New Bedford,... 29 81
Collection, St. Paul's, Boston .. 133 28
Chandler, Obiel.................. 20
Children of Rev. Mr. Boyd's congregation, Philadelphia. 6
Children of Rev. Mr. Allen's congregation, Philadelphia. 5
Collection in Philadelphia, for Kenyon College, and handed by Rev. B. Allen to Bishop Chase, May 24, 1827......... 304 27
Clergyman from Vermont...... 2
Cash........................... 1
Clay, Henry................... 50
Chapman, George............... 3
Coxe, J. R., family of............ 5
Corke, J. H., " Fluvenna, Va................................ 5
Cowper, M. A., Savannah...... 5
Chatham, Joseph.................. 1
Chase, Dudley.................. 200
Chase, Mrs. Olivia.............. 20
Chase, Baruch.................. 61
Chase, Mrs. Ellen.............. 25
Colt, Thomas, Salem, Mass... 25
Chase, B...................... 5
Dehon, Madam, Charleston, S. C........................... 10
Dupuy, Rev. C. M., Phila. 10
Dunlap, Miss Ann, Philadel'a. 5
Douglass, Miss " 5
Dawson, George, " 5
Dundas, Mr. " 10
Delancy, Rev. W. H. " 5
Duche, Mrs. " 10
Downing, J. W. " 5
Depeyster, James F., N. York. 25
Depeyster, R. G. B. " 10
Depeyster, F. A. " 10
Depeyster, Fred, Jr. " 10
Depeyster, Abraham, " 10
Depeyster, Frederick, " 50
Dominick, Jas. " 20
Dorr, Sullivan, Providence, R. I........................... 20
D. C., Portland.................. 5
Daniel, Otis, Boston. 10
Dodge, Mrs. Catherine, " 5
Dix, Stephen A. " 10
Daniel, Josiah, " 3
Davidson, Thomas T. " 5
Dunn, James C. " 20
Denison, Dr., Royalton, Vt.... 50
Drummond, Mr., in behalf of several subscribers in Washington City................. 20
Denison, Mrs. Rachel............ 16
Elmes, Thomas, Philadelphia. 10
Eldred, Miss, " 1

Ebright, Lydia, Philadelphia.$ 5
Eaton, Rev. A., Boston......... 100
Ely, Mr., of Rochester......... 10
Elmer, E., Bridgton, N. J...... 5
" Episcopalian," N. Carolina. 1
Edson, E. Waymouth, Md...... 5
Fortune, James.................. 3
Farr, John, Philadelphia. 50
Friend, by Rev. — Allen. " 5
Friend, " 20
Feinor, G. " 5
Feltus, Rev. Dr., New York. 50
Friend, by Mr. Okie, " 25
Friend to the cause, by Mr. Edwards.................... 20
Friend by Mr. K.............. 20
Friend to the cause, by A. Cushman................. 10
Farnham, Miss, Boston......... 10
Friends, Portland, 10, 5, 5, 5, 3, 3, 2, 2, 2, 3, 3............ 43
Friend, by Mr. Newton......... 10
Fullerton, Boston.............. 25
Fullerton, of Blank............ 10
Friend, by Mr. Lowden........ 5
Friend, by Mrs. Wilson...... 10
Friend, by Mr. Clark.......... 10
Fullerton, W. J................ 5
Friend, by G. Hoyt............. 50
Fuller, Dr., Beaufort, S. C., on Mr. Bacon's subscription, paid N. R. Bank, N. Y., Sep., 1829, of the following subscribers:
   Mrs. Mary Jenkins... $28
   Rev. Wm. Walker... 10
   Mrs. Mary Barnwell, 15
   Miss E. Barnwell..... 20
   Miss Ann Barnwell.. 20
   Mr. Wm. Barnwell... 5
   Miss Obrian.......... 10
   Dr. Fuller............. 10 115
Foster, J. & S, Andover, Mass. 5
Few Friends, by Rev. Dr. Cairns, Alexandria, D. C.... 10
Friends, in Boston, by Rev. Eaton.......................... 5
Friend, Brooklyn............... 2
Gentleman, by a Lady, Philadelphia........................ 5
Gardiner, Mr., Philadelphia... 5
Garwood, Mrs. " 2
Griffith, Rob't E. " 5
Gebhard and Mrs. Halverstadt, 10
Grey, John & Co., N. Y......... 3
Goddard, William, Providence, R. I............................ 5
G., Mr., Portland, Me.......... 7
Goddard, A.................... 5
Gibbs, Miss, Boston............ 100
Green, William 25
Green, Charles W.............. 10

Green, Miss, by Mr. Clark, Boston	$10
Greenleaf, Samuel, Boston.....	25
Grant, Moses, "	10
Gilbert, Samuel, "	5
Green, Gardner, "	100
Gray, Miss Agnes, Va.........	5
Gray, H. N., "	10
Greenleaf, Charlotte K., Va...	2
Greenleaf, Simon, Portland...	15
Gibbons, Thomas, N. Y	50
Gardiner, Emma..................	3
Grammer, Rev. John..........	5
Gill, Robert, N. Y..............	10
Gregory, Walter, Troy.	3
Hutchens, Mr. and Miss, Phila.	20
Hughes, Miss, "	20
Henry, Alexander, "	50
Hale & Davidson, "	20
Hance, Conrad, "	10
Hemphill, Joseph, "	10
Huddle, Joseph, "	10
Hutton, Miss, "	1
Hemphill, Joseph, second subscription, Philadelphia......	40
Hawkins, George, "	3
Hutchinson, R....................	5
Higley, Virginia	2
Hunter, John, Radnor........	10
Hunter, Miss Ann "	5
Holland, Mrs. "	5
Hill, John, N. Y...........	20
Hartman, Mr. "	5
Hone, Philip "	50
Hillyer, Philo "	15
Haight, H. E. "	20
Halsey, Thomas L., Prov., R. I.	100
Hoppin, John, Sutton...........	5
Hollister, Miss, Boston......	1
Holmes & Homer "	30
Hubbard, Samuel "	10
Head, F. C.	10
H. H. Henry, ...	20
Howard, B. "	20
Haman, William "	5
Hawley, Rev. William, collected in Washington City..	200
Hawley, Rev. William...........	10
H., New York	5
Hanse, Conrad, Philadelphia..	5
Hall, Daniel, Troy............	5
Humphrey, Hector, Cohen.....	1
Hartford, Parishioner..........	1
Huntington, Mr. and Mrs., of Natchez......................	15
ingersol, C. J., Philadelphia,	10
Jones, William "	20
Janney, Dr. "	5
Johnston, A. W. "	5
Jarvis, Mrs. Bishop "	5
James, Dr. "	10
Jones Isaac, New York......	20

Jenkins, Jas., New York......	$10	
Jauncy, Mr. "	30	
Jay, John "	100	
Ingraham, Henry E."	25	
Ives, Thomas, Providence, R.I.	20	
Jones, Alexander " "	20	
Jeffrey, John, Boston...........	10	
Ingalls, William "	10	
Ingle, John P., Washington...	10	
ingle, Edward " ...	5	
J. H. G., Boston................	2	
Janney, Benjamin S., Phila...	20	
Jay, William, Bedford........	1	
Jackson, Rev. and Rev. Mr. Lippitt	10	
Ibbotson, Henry, of Sheffield, England...................	20	
Jones, W	10	
Ingraham, Mrs. S....	5	
Johnson, Rev. M. H., Park, New York.......	25	
Janson, John, Kingston, N. Y.	10	
Klapp, Dr. Joseph, Phila.......	5	
Kuhl, H. "	20	
Kitchens, Misses "	10	
Kirkham, William "	20	
Kip, Leonard "	50	
Kenyon Circle, Portland......	50	
Kenyon Circle, Newburyport,	55	
Knapp, Charles, Boston.........	5	
Kenyon Circle, Gardiner.	70	
Kenyon Circle, Newburyport,	50	
Keith, Rev. Dr.............	10	
Kenyon Circle, Newburyport,	10	
" " "	15	
Kellogg, Rev. E. B..............	10	
Kellogg, Edmond............ ..	10	
Kenyon College, an early friend of..........................	1	
Lady, young, Philadelphia.....	1	50
Lady, "	5	
Lady, by Mr. Allen..............	5	
Lott, Mrs........		50
Lady, by Rev. Dr. Hutchin...	5	
Lex, Jacob, by Mr. Biddle.....	15	
Lewis, M. M................	5	
Littell, Mr....................	5	
Lady of St. Andrew's Church,	5	
Little Girl........................		50
Lady, by Mr. Carter......	2	
Lewis, Lawrence.............	10	
Leiper, William J............	5	
Lady, widow, of Jamaica, L. I.	20	
Lady, by Mr. Clark............	7	
Lady, by Mrs. Odenymer......	1	
Lady (J.), N. Y............	100	
Lorillard, George "	100	
Low, John "	25	
Lee, Gideon "	50	
Ladies, unknown "	9	
Lawrence, Amos, Boston,	9	
Lady, by Rev. Mr. Eaton, "	20	

Lady, by Rev. Mr. Eaton,
Boston............................... $10
" " " " 8
" Newburyport............. 3
" Portland, Maine......... 1
" by Mr. Potter, Boston... 4
Lamson, John A. " .. 10
Lathrop, Miss S. " ... 5
Ladies of Emmanuel's Church,
Bellows Falls, Vermont..... 33
Lady, by Mrs. Eaton, Boston.. 10
Lady, by Miss Bell............. 10
Lady, T. Clark.................... 1
Lawrence, Abbot.................. 50
Locke, Ephraim.................. 10
Livingston, E. P., N. Y......... 25
Loring, Dr. B...................... 25
Leonard, Rev. George, N. H... 10
Lewis, Edward.................... 2
Lawrence, J. B., Salem, Mass. 1
Leonard, Rev. George.......... 5
Lee, H., Virginia................. 10
Lightfoot, Walker, Virginia... 1
Ladies of Charlestown " ... 35
Lady, unknown, to Mr. Kip,
New York......................... 150
Lockwood, Miss, New York... 2
Mackenzie, Philadelphia...... 30
McKinly, John, Philadelphia, 5
Morgan, Mrs. Mary " 5
" " " Jr. " 5
Milne, Richard " 20
Meredith, W. " 10
Myers, Mrs. " 5
McAlester, Charles " 10
Miller, Jun. " 3
Montgomery, Joseph " 10
Maryland friend.................. 10
Matlock, Mrs..................... 5
Member of St. Paul's, N. Y.... 3
Marsh, David " ... 10
Murray, Misses " ... 100
M., Mrs., Newburyport......... 2 20
Mallet, E. J., Providence, R. I. 5
Mabbit, Mrs. M., Troy, N. Y... 122
McLean, Mrs., Boston.......... 25
Maynard, Elias " 5
Monroe, Edmund " 10
McNeil, Sarah " 2
McLeary, Mrs. F. S. " 5
Martin, James, Washington... 5
McLean, J. " ... 15
Morsell, J. S., D. C.............. 10
Minor, Mrs. Lucy, Virginia... 30
Munn, John, Hartford, Conn. 1
Merrick, Joseph F., Md........ 1
McFarland, Wm., Worcester,
Massachusetts.................. 1
Meade, Mr. D., Fred. co., Va. 5
Minn, Mr. L...................... 10
Maxwell, Miss S. A............. 10
Milnor, Rev. Dr., to Mr. Kip.. 50

Milnor, Rev. Dr......... ....$100
McGuire, Rev. E., collected of
sundry persons, Fred'bg, Va. 30
Mintzer, Rev. G., collected in
Pennsylvania, of the fol-
lowing persons:
Buel, L........ ......$10
Douglas, Geo....... 5
Jacobs, Cyrus...... 50
Jenkins, Robt...... 3
Dennis, Edward... 3
Brooks, Clement... 5
Hinton, Isaac...... 5
Smith, Mrs.......... 10
Reim, B............. 10
Yates, Mrs......... 30
Beers, D.... 3
Hopkins, H. J 10
Cash................ 61 12
                    ————
                    $205 12
Deduct Mr. Mint-
zer's expenses.. 30 00
Leaving a balance of——— 175 12
Nassan & Benevan, Philadel-
phia............ 5
Negus, Stephen, Philadelphia. 40
New York Episcopalian......... 20
Noble, Mr. L., New York....... 5
Noble, Mrs. " 25
Nixon, Mrs. C. " 5
Nichols, John.................... 10
Nixon, Mrs., 2d donation...... 5
Norris, John, of Hewingdon
Hall, Bucks, Eng............. ... 24 44
One of St. Peter's Congrega-
tion, Pa........................... 5
Ogle, Mr., Philadelphia 5
Otis Norcross & Co., Boston... 5
Oakley, Peter..................... 10
Poulson, Mrs., Philadelphia.... 20
Poor woman, " 5
Puchin, John C. " 5
Pratt, Henry, " 20
Patterson, Rev. N. " 5
Pechin, Christiana, " 20
Patterson, Jonat'n, " 5
Phillips, W. " 10
Pearce, Cromwell, " 10
Perrott, J., N. Y.................. 3
Park, Robert C., N. Y........... 20
Poor woman, by Dr. Milnor,
N. Y............................... 1
Pintard, John, N. Y............. 25
Prince, N. " 50
Platt................................ 10
Perkins, J. W..................... 100
Pell, Mrs., N. Y.................. 20
Peet, for the S. S. Teachers
St. George's Church........... 61 25
Prouty, Mrs. Boston 5
Perkins, Madam, Boston........ 100

Parker, M. S., Boston............	$10
Portsmouth, N. H., by Rev. C. Burroughs	152
Parsons, Gorham, Boston......	20
Parker, James D. "	20
Peters, Edward, "	25
Powell, Mrs. Catherine, Bost..	30
Pollock, Fred. J., Virginia.....	5
Perkins, James, Boston.........	50
Parx, D. "	5
Perry, Mrs., New Bedford......	2
Prout, Robert, Char. Co., Md..	5
Peet, Fred., M	1
Parker, W. S., Troy..	5
Robbins, John, Philadelphia...	5
Ralston, Robert, " ...	50
Ralston, A. G. " ...	5
Rankin, William, " ...	50
Riley, J. S. " ...	5
Robert, Seth, " ...	5
Rogers, David, N. Y.............	20
Robins, John, "	50
Rogers, by W. Clark............	5
Reynolds, W. B. "	20
Ragan, Richard, Md.............	1
Raynolds, Dr., of Boston.......	10
Rings, gold, two...	4 50
Sawyer, James, Philadelphia..	5
Stanley, Norris, "	10
Sergeant, Mrs. Gov. "	100
Stanley, N. W. "	5
Stephenson, W. "	50
Stiles, T. T., by Mr. Allen	5
Smith. Edward, "	5
Saunders, Mr. "	2
Stevenson, Cornelius, "	20
Stokes, James, "	25
Sergeant, Mrs. J. "	5
Smith, W. P. "	1
Swift, Miss Mary, "	10
Sperry, Jacob, "	5
Smith, Thomas H. "	100
Sigourney, Chas., Hartford, Ct.	100
Swan, B. L., N. Y...............	100
Spooner, H. "	100
Sands, Joseph......	30
Sands, Miss......	2
Simpson, Mary, N. Y............	3
Stuyvesant, P. G. "	100
Suffern, Thomas, "	25
Searle, Nathaniel, Prov., R. I..	10
Slater, Samuel, Oxford, Mass.	100
Stoddard, Charles, Boston......	10
Safford, Daniel, "	5
Simpson, F. H........	3
Sowden	100
Stimpson, William C., Boston..	10
Sowden, John, Jr. "	5
Shepherd, R. D. "	20
Stone, Mrs., by Mr. Kip.........	3
Smallwood, W. A., Washington	25
Shepherd, Moses...	5

Sargeant, Mrs.......	$5	
Steele, R., Abington........	1	
Sigourney, Mrs...................	1	
Sprigg, D., Md....................	1	
Smith, George A., Va............	2	
Seeley, Miss, New Haven......	5	
Her pupils........	5	
Sprague, of Ramapo, N. Y.....	20	
Stokes, W., Philadelphia........	10	
Taylor, Bankson, "	50	
Tryon, George, "	50	
Thompson, Walter, Phil'a......	5	
Thurston, Miss, "	50	
Teacher and two pupils of a Bible Class of St. Peter's Church, Philadelphia.........	1	75
Thompson, J. C...................	5	
Tyng, Rev. S. H., of Maryland	10	
Townsend, Mr., New York.....	5	
Tracy, Frederick A. "	25	
Tappan, Arthur, "	100	
T., Mrs. "	10	
T., Mr. "	10	
Teachers, St. George's Church.	25	
Thompson, Thos., Prov., R. I...	10	
Tillinghast, J. L. " ...	5	
Ten Broeck, Rev. M., Portland	25	
Titcomb & Butler, "	10	
Tappan, John, Boston...........	80	
Thorndike, Israel, "	50	
Tyng, Rev. Stephen.............	10	
Tyngey, Commodore......	50	
Todd, Mr..........	1	
Thorn, Reuben T., by Mrs. Gray	7	
Townsend, Henry, Troy.........	1	
Urquhart, W., Buck co..........	10	
Van Wagenen, Hubert, N. Y..	10	
Varrick, Richard, "	50	
Vinton, A. M., Providence.....	3	
Wagner, T. & S., Philadelphia	10	
Weir, Silas E. "	10	
Wallington, Capt. "	5	
Watson, Charles C. "	5	
Watson, Henry R. "	5	
Wacksmuth, "	5	
Wheeler, Enoch, "	5	
Waldburgh, Mrs. "	5	
Whilden, Capt. "	3	
Walton, Mr., New York.......	3	
Walton, Miss, "	3	
Wooley, B. L. "	25	
Wilson, William, "	25	
Wright, Mrs. Wm., Newark, N. J......	10	
Watts, Dr., New York...........	25	
Willis, Wm. F. "	5	
Williams, Mrs. Sarah T., N. Y.	100	
Warner, E. "	15	
Ward, Mrs. and Miss, Providence, R. I......	2	
Wood, J. B., Prov., R. I.........	100	

Waste, Stephen, Portland	$5	Well-wisher	$2
Wigglesworth, E., Boston	5	White, Adam	1
Walcott, N. D. "	5	Wooster, Rev. T., Salisbury,	
Weld, Mrs. J. "	5	N. H.,	1
Wyatt, Mr.	5	Well-wisher, Hillsborough	1
Wheelwright, Lot..	20	Ward, James, 2d subscription.	5
Ward, James, Hartford	5	Ward, Mrs., Hartford	10
Widow's offering, Kingston	5	Woodward, Rachel, O.	1
Wilson, John, Boston	100	Zabriskie, A. C., N. Y.	10

The following names were inadvertently omitted in the alphabetical arrangement by Bishop Chase, and it seems best now to preserve his arrangement:

Bunce, Geo., N. Y.	$1	Friend, New Haven	$3
Fogg, Mrs., Brooklyn, Ct.	5	Fogg, Elizabeth, Brooklyn, Ct.	1
Friends in Albany, signed		Forrest, Rev. Mr., Stamford,	
"Connecticut"	5	N. Y.	2
Friends, several, Raleigh, N.		Friend W. (unknown), Baltimore	5
C.	5		
Friend, Bedford, Penn.	1	Friend, Washington City	2
Friends, two, by J. M. M	10	Twells, Mrs..	50

SUBSCRIPTIONS TO KENYON COLLEGE IN THE PARISH AT WEST RIVER, MD., MARCH, 1827.

Thomas G. Hall	$5 00
Rinaldo Prindell	3 00
Charles Hodges	5 00
Henry A. Hall	5 00
Robert H. McPherson	2 00
Mrs. Priscilla Prindall	5 00
Mrs. C. Lansdale	5 00
	——— $30

The above was subscribed to E. Bacon, and collected by John Sellman, Esq., Feb. 18, 1828.

From the Rev. G. H. Jones, of Smithfield, Va. (an old subscription lately paid)	5
From Mrs. Hepburn, of Milton, Pa., per Wm. Stickney	5
Remaining in my hands, from former collections	10
	——— $50

P. S. The above-named fifty dollars was sent to Mr. Kip by the Rev. Mr. Hall.

Yours most respectfully,   E. BACON.

LAST OF CONTRIBUTIONS TO KENYON COLLEGE FROM HARTFORD, CONNECTICUT, 1828.

	In Money.	Cloth.	Work.	Books.
Mrs. Ward,	$1 00	$2 00		
Mrs. Bartholomew,		2 00		
Mrs. Brainard,		2 00		
Mrs. Nichols,	1 00			
Mrs. M. N. Beach,	1 00			
Mrs. C. Tousy,	1 00			
Mrs. S. Griswold,	1 00			
Mrs. Sigourney,	7 00		5 00	4 00

By the exertions of a Reverend brother in the City of Philadelphia,* the late appeal made by me has resulted in several donations, amounting to $400 actually received. By advices from that brother of late date, I understand that $100 additional may be expected soon, and a still further sum of $100 promised at a longer period. For this whole sum we are to be indebted to the congregation of St. Andrew's Church, $200 of which is from a society of ladies, the result of their own work.

N. B. If in the multiplicity of cares, the Bishop has omitted to insert the name of any donor, (in which the Seminary would be the loser,) or any donation has been twice acknowledged, by being included in any aggregate sum, and also set down separately in the above list, (in which case the Bishop would be loser,) it is earnestly requested that such mistake be immediately communicated for correction.—*Bishop Chase's Pamphlet*, 1829.

ST. GEORGE'S CHURCH SCHOLARSHIP.

In addition to the above, it should be stated, that St. George's Church paid into the treasury of the Institution, $1,000, in consideration of which, that Church was forever to have the privilege of keeping, at Kenyon, a student for the ministry, at the charge of the Institution for board, tuition, washing, fuel, and lights, during the forty weeks of term time. This could have been done at that time, when the charges for these items in College were only $70, but it would be a hard bargain if enforced now, when these bills are more than doubled.

MILNOR PROFESSORSHIP.

Respecting this professorship very little can be ascertained. Dr. Tyng writes that he knows nothing of its origin. From statements

---

* Rev. B. Allen.

made incidentally by Bishop Chase, at different times, it appears that Arthur Tappan, of New York, originated the movement by offering $1,000, provided $10,000 should be subscribed. Bishop Chase contributed $1,000; but who made up the balance, can not now be ascertained. There were some failures of subscription, and Bishop Chase's gift was absorbed in the treasury; so that when Bishop Chase resigned, the fund in the hands of the New York trustees was considerably less than $10,000. This has since been made up by St. George's Church contributing $2,500.

This fund is under the entire control of trustees appointed by the vestry of St. George's Church, the interest of which, according to the conditions of the subscription, was forever to be applied to the support of the "Milnor Professor of Systematic Divinity in the Theological Seminary of the Diocese of Ohio."

The nomination of the incumbent was to be made by the Rector of St. George's Church during the life of Dr. Milnor, and ten years afterward.

Those who have given these funds will here very naturally inquire how they have been expended. In this respect, very little was at the option of Bishop Chase. In building an institution of learning amid a dense forest, the first thing to be done would be to hire workmen and build shanties for them to live in. In the absence of markets, and amid a very sparse squatter population, lands must be cleared and grounds tilled to afford workmen the means of living. As nothing in the way of building could be done without lumber, and this could not be had in sufficient quantities at any reasonable price, mills must be erected for its manufacture. For this, too, heavy ox teams, and all the costly appliances of hauling saw-logs and lumber must be provided. A flouring mill was also needed to furnish material for the staff of life. Thus, in almost every particular after Gambier was chosen, it was necessary to begin with the very elements of civilization.

But the Institution must soon be in operation, that funds might be coming in, and a right influence going out; and yet the first buildings for the use of students must, from the brief time allowed, nearly all be temporary. To erect such, would be the dictate of prudence and sound judgment; but in this case it was necessity, which knows no law. Nearly all the buildings that Bishop Chase erected, at an expense nearly equal to the amount of what was collected in this country, were temporary, and have since entirely disappeared. The whole amount collected by Bishop Chase, in the United States, was about $18,000, and the cost of buildings that were temporary, of clearing and fencing farms, and farming stock and implements, was put down by him, in 1830, at $17,217.

The balance of the $30,000 obtained in Europe, after paying for the land, was also invested in building, and a considerable debt incurred besides, which was afterward paid by the sale of lands. But Bishop Chase's works were not all temporary. The central part of the building, known as Kenyon College, 110 feet by 40, with walls of stone four feet in thickness at the base, was built by him, and will stand while time shall last, a fitting monument of such a man as Bishop Chase. The foundation, also, of Rosse Chapel was laid by him, and above $3,000 expended upon it; but upon a plan entirely different from the one afterward adopted, when it was built with funds solicited by Bishop McIlvaine.

The Institution was thus brought in debt, which was afterward liquidated by a sale of the north half of the original purchase. A circumstance ought to be mentioned here, to elicit information. Bishop Chase says, in his defense, page fifteen : "Seventeen lots and out-lots are bargained away and paid for;" but what particular lots they were, and who purchased them, has not been ascertained. The sum of $1,310, received on this account, was acknowledged by Bishop Chase. No deeds were ever given, and the money must have been intended rather as a donation than as the price of a purchase, else the trustees would have been asked to refund.

The following communication of Philander Chase Freeman, Esq., and found in the "*Statistics of the Philomathesian Society*," p. 27, gives a vivid idea of what Gambier was at the time here referred to:

"When I first entered Kenyon, then located at Worthington, Ohio was in its infancy, and its inhabitants not much advanced in knowledge or even civilization. My first years at Kenyon were spent in a log cabin for my study. I went to Gambier before the College was erected, and before any improvements were made on the College Hill. The first night I spent on the College Hill, was in a cabin of boughs, covered with English blankets, the donation of

English liberality, while the foundations of Kenyon College were being laid. In the winter of 1827, I was engaged in teaching the first rudiments of the English language to original settlers, in a log cabin, situated about forty rods north-west of the College building, on the banks of 'Owl creek,' alias Vernon river. I spent three months of the winter of 1828, in Perry township, teaching the good people's children. My terms of tuition were $2,00 per scholar for three months, payable in corn at ten cents per bushel, and wheat at twenty-five cents per bushel. I had a school of eighty scholars and upward. My recompense in corn and wheat all went to Kenyon to pay for my board and tuition. The College was not completed to receive inhabitants till about three months before I received my degree; consequently, during all my college course, I lived in temporary buildings, except three months."

BISHOP CHASE'S DEFENSE.

After Bishop Chase returned from England, one G. M. West insinuated himself into the good graces of Lords Kenyon and Gambier, and came to this country upon their recommendation, for the purpose of receiving Holy Orders. Soon after his ordination, West, under the title of Chaplain to the Bishop of Ohio, went to England, to superintend the further collection of funds for Kenyon College. After his return to this country in 1830, it not only appeared that he was entirely unworthy of confidence himself, but he originated the most grievous charges against Bishop Chase. This, though painful, was most opportune. The dollars from "friends," in answer to the Bishop's earnest appeal, began to be few and far between. Kenyon still needed funds, and unless some untoward event had occurred, Bishop Chase even would have been at a loss what to do. But now he so completely vindicated himself and his acts, in a pamphlet addressed to Dr. Milnor, that many of his "friends" thought it time to send him another "*dollar*." Accordingly, the following sums were received during the years 1830 and 1831.

SUBSCRIPTIONS SENT IN ANSWER TO BISHOP CHASE'S DEFENSE.

Adams, Demas, Columbus, O.	$ 25
American, Brighton, Eng.	50
Anonymous, P. Mills, Md......	5
Army Officer of, West Point...	10
Bull, Rev. Levi, Lancaster, Pa...........	100
Caswell, Henry, Gambier......	3
Cady, D. K., Cincinnati, O.....	5
Cadle, R. F., Green Bay........	5
Carter, Misses, St. Clairsville	4
Circle St. Paul's Church, Chillicothe	10
Cleveland, Geo., Charleston, S. C.........	100
Comstock, Mrs., New Canaan, Ct.........	5
Cooke, Dr., Lexington, Ky.....	9
Corning, Jasper, Charleston, S. C.........	100
Denison, Mrs. J., Royalton, Vt.	20
Devalt, Joseph..................	1
Dinwiddie Co., Va., in a letter	20
Douglas, Archibald, Gambier..	1
Ducachet, Rev. H. W., Philadelphia	10
Eggleston, G. W., Charleston, S. C.........	20
Ely, Miss Sarah, N. Y.........	10
Foote, C., Middletown, Ct......	5
Friend, Carlisle, Pa...........	5
Friend, Stratford, Ct.......	5
Gray, Agnes, Traveler's Rest, Va.	5
Gray, Margaret.................	5
Greenleaf, Simon, Portland, Me.	5
Grimke, Thomas S., Charleston, S. C.........	50
Hall, David, Pomfret, Ct.......	1
Hogg, Mr. Geo., Brownsville, Pa.........	10
Hopkins, Rev. John H., Pittsburg.........	10
Jacobs, Miss Ann, Charlestown, Pa.........	20
Jay, William, Bedford, N. Y.	15
Johnson, Rev. Mr., per Rev. Mr. Rogers, N. Y.	50

Johnson, F., Fredericksburg, Va.	$ 10
Kost, Mrs., Stratford, Ct.......	5
Kellogg, Josiah, Troy, N. Y....	25
Ladies, Trinity Church, and St. Paul's Chapel, N. Y..........	150
Ladies, Newark, O..............	10
Ladies, Zanesville, O...........	20
Ladies, Delaware, O............	10
Lord, Miss Mary, N. Y.........	5
McDowell, Abraham, Columbus, O.........	10
Mark, N. J., Philadelphia......	20
Meade, Bishop, and a few Friends	50
Minor, J. Mercer, legacy of, Va.........	25
Muenscher, Reverend Joseph, Northampton, Mass.	5
Parker, Mr. J., Esq., Perth Amboy, N. J.	14
Parkers' Little Children.........	11
Putnam, David, Marietta......	5
Ralston, Mrs. E., Philadelphia	18
Shaffer, Michael.........	1
Shepherd, Rev. G., Stratford, Ct.........	5
Shepherd, Mrs................	15
Sigourney, C., Hartford.........	10
Smith, Mrs. A., Gambier, O....	5
Smith, Mrs. E., Milton, N. C.	5
St. James, Zanesville vestry...	15
St. Paul's, Chillicothe vestry..	65
Stough, Dr., New Philadelphia, O.........	8
Stratton, Rev. S. C., Snow Hill, Md.........	10
Thorn, Reuben T., Fredericksburg, Va.	5
Thompson, Dr. John, Kanawha, Va..................	5
Trinity, Cleveland, by Rev. J. McElroy	20
Unknown, Brunswick, Va.....	10
Wilcox, P. B., Columbus, O....	50
Total...............	$1,291 25

SUBSCRIPTIONS TO KENYON COLLEGE OBTAINED IN THE SPRING OF 1831, BY MESSRS. DEXTER POTTER, OF CAMBRIDGE, MASS., AND J. P. B. WILMER, OF PHILADELPHIA.

ST. CLAIRSVILLE, O.			
Miss Carter......	$ 5	Mr. P. Tallman	$ 5
Judge Ruggles..	31	MORRISTOWN.	
Mr. Inskeep....	10	Noble Taylor	50

WHEELING, VA.

John Robinson	$ 5
Joseph Morrison	1
Wm. Dulty	2
Mrs. Lyon	1
Delaplaine	1
P. G. Stephenson	1
J. Armstrong	1
Thomas Jones	3
J. W. Stone	1
J. B. Curtis	5
J. F. Clock	5
J. Miller	2

BROWNSVILLE, PA.

Jacob Bowman	30
Isabella Bowman	20
Mary A. Hogg	10
James L. Bowman	5
Henry Sweitzer	5
G. H. Bowman	10
William Hogg	10
D. N. Robinson	3
Eliza Robinson	2
Robert Clark	10
Rev. Wm. Bowman	10
Cash	2

SNOW HILL, MD.

J. C. Handy	5	
William Parnel	5	
William Porter	1	
Dr. L. D. Handy	2	
J. J. Taylor	2	
Charles Parnel	2	
Cash	1	
L. P. Spencer	2	50
Thomas L. Disharoom	2	
C. K. Wilson	2	50
Mrs. Amanda Robins	10	
Mrs. Sarah Sturges		50
Wm. Le Compte		50
Rev. Mr. Stratton's Bible Class	2	50
L. Townsend	2	
Samuel G. Cluff	1	
Ann Johnson		50
Thomas R. Spencer	2	

PRINCESS ANN, MD.

W. W. Johnson	5	
L. T. White	1	
George A. Deshiel	5	
J. H. Bell	1	
Mrs. Sarah Hayward	5	
Littleton Long	1	
Samuel Holbrook		50
William Walles		50
J. White	1	
Mrs. M. C. Jones	1	
John Jones	1	
Jesse Hugher	5	
J. N. Bowland	1	

Mathias Mills	$	50
J. H. King		50
Mrs. H. Saddler	1	
J. Stewart	1	
Miss L. M. Stewart	1	
J. W. Dore	1	
L. Waters and Geo. Dashiels	2	
L. P. and S. Dennis	6	50
S. Dorsey and G. Wetter	1	
Rev. G. McIlhenny	1	

SALISBURY, MD.

B. Deshiel	2
Jehu Parsons	10
Elijah Parsons	10
Charles Leary, of Vienna	5

HAGERSTOWN, MD.

D. Sprigg	10
O. Lawrence	10
Dr. Magee	5

HANCOCK, MD.

Names not sent	25

BERLIN, MD.

J. Covington	1
G. Parnell	10
J. C. Marshall	1
S. E. Mees	1
J. B. Robins	1
James Robins	1
J. J. Poynter	1
J. C. Dunson	1
James Dunson	1
L. J. Parnell	1
J. W. Williams	1

GEORGETOWN, D. C.

P. Robinson	5	
J. Honis	2	
Charles Junell	1	
C. Leyton, $2, Cash, $1	3	
Com. Poynter	2	
M. Reuch	1	
J. Richards	1	
P. Johnson	2	
Mrs. Emerson	2	
Miss G. Phillips	5	
G. Hickman, Lewistown	5	
Cash "	5	
M. Burton, Darborough	5	
H. M. Ridgeley, Dover, Del	5	
Mrs. Ridgeley	2	50
M. Lockerman	2	
Sundry persons	7	50
H. Hudson, Milford	2	
Cash "		25
C. Ridgely, Smyrna, Del	2	
W. Holding, $1, W. Daniel, $2,	3	
H. H. Lockwood	1	50
D. Clayton, 50c., J. Jones, 50c.	1	

A. Dickson, 25, W. Woolls, 25, $	50	W. Naffish.......................... $	50
Cash...	50	B. Coombe...........................	2
E. Clock......................................	1	Jabez Cumings................	10
A. Ford.......................................	1	Ann Wilson.................. ...	1
M. Savin.....................................	50	From D. Potter, in a letter	
C. W. Hale.................................	1	dated Cambridge, Mass......	22
R. C. Johnson............................	50		
D. Cowly....................................	50		$535 25
Dr. Lockwood...........................	50		

SUMMARY.

The amount received by the Institution, through the hands of Bishop Chase, as nearly as can at present be ascertained, is as follows :

English Donations..	$ 30,000 00
Collected in Ohio...	3,298 96
Collected in the United States, exclusive of Ohio.........	12,276 65
Mr. Hogg, deduction on land......................................	6,000 00
St. George's Church Scholarship.................................	1,000 00
Bishop Chase's donation to Milnor Professorship, paid into the Treasury...	1,000 00
Donation of Bishop Chase for Residence......................	1,000 00
Milnor Fund, in the hands of New York Trustees............	7,148 00
Received for Cornish lots...	1,310 00
Answer to Bishop Chase's Defense..............................	1,291 24
Result of Potter & Wilmer's Agency............................	535 25
	64,856 10
Deduct expenses of Printing and Agencies, at least...	856 10
	$64,000 00

Thus closes the record of Bishop Chase's labors, and their results, in founding a Theological Seminary and College. He probably had no superior in all the qualities necessary to originate such an institution. The versatility of his manners was such, that he could adapt himself readily to any condition of society. Whether he were in the log cabin of Ohio, where the whole family slept, ate, cooked, received guests and lodged them, in the same apartment, or in the magnificent halls of Lord Kenyon, surrounded with the refinement of the old world, Bishop Chase was equally at home, and capable of winning golden opinions. Add to this an energy that never flagged, a will that never succumbed, and a physical system that never tired, and we have such a character as is seldom produced, but which was precisely adapted to the great work that he accomplished. Bishop Chase was equally remarkable for industry and endurance. Daylight seldom found him in bed, and he seemed as fond of working or traveling in the rain, as though water were his native element. He would preach at Perry, fifteen miles from Gambier, and as soon as daylight peeped in the East on Monday morning, take his bridle himself, go to the field, catch Cincinnatus, mount and be off to set his head-men at work in Gambier. Bishop Chase began a work for the Church in Ohio, and in truth for the whole West, such as no other man then living would have attempted, or probably could have accomplished.

Bishop McIlvaine's Appeal for Funds in 1833.

In 1832 Bishop McIlvaine undertook the care of the Diocese and Seminary. The first step necessary to put the Institution in a working condition, was to provide the means of erecting buildings. All except the one college edifice, 110 by 40, and the kitchen part of one professors's residence, were temporary structures, and have since entirely disappeared. After Bishop Chase left, and before Bishop McIlvaine came, something had been done in the way of building, but nothing to provide means, except the sale of lands; and the avails of these were needed to pay debts. In truth, as yet, only the foundation of the Seminary was laid. The superstructure must be reared. For this Bishop McIlvaine made an appeal to his friends, and the friends of the Church, in the East. The following is the result:

Subscriptions to the Theological Seminary of the Diocese of Ohio, to aid in the Erection of New Buildings, obtained by the Rt. Rev. C. P. McIlvaine, D. D., in 1833.

NEW YORK.		
Allen, Moses	$100	
Adriane, Elizabeth	2	
Anderson, Abel J.	200	
Ascension Church Bible Class,	200	
Ascension Church Ben. Soc.	73 09	
Aspinwall, W. H.	50	
Baker, L.	50	
Benjamin, W. M.	10	
Bethune, Mrs.	10	
Blackstock, Mr.	50	
Bolton, Thomas.	50	
Boorman, I.	250	
Brewster, I. & L.	100	
By same.	5	
Bricher, Walter.	50	
Brown, James	$ 50	
Brown, Stewart	200	
Bruen, G. W.	200	
Burtus, James	200	
Carey, Mr. H.	200	
Cash, 4 donations	52	
Chester, W. W.	200	
Chadwick, Wm. A.	100	
Crary, J. S.	50	
Crosby, W. B.	500	
Codwise, Mrs. David	50	
Codwise, David	50	
Codwise, Mrs. George	10	
Coit, Levi	50	
Corning, Jasper	50	
Corning & Walker	25	

Couch, William	$ 50
Curtis, Walter M.	1
Dennison, John	50
Dominick, James M.	20
Donaldson, Robert	100
Douglas, George	50
Dyson, Robert	200
Eastburn, Rev. M.	200
Edgerton, Mr.	15
Erban, Henry	25
Faile, Thomas H.	25
Ferguson, John	50
Few, Mrs.	100
Fox, G. F.	50
Francis, Dr.	50
Gardiner, Mr.	11
Gracie, Archibald	50
Griffin	10
Griswold, George	100
Haines, Richard J.	100
Halsted, Mr.	50
Hoffner, L. M.	100
Holden, Horace	25
Holmes, Obadiah	200
Holmes, Silas	100
Howland, S. S.	100
Hoyt, James J.	100
Jackson, Rev. Wm.	100
Jaggar, Jehiel, jr.	25
Jaggart, Mrs. Ann M.	25
Jay, William	25
Jay, Peter A.	50
Jones, W. K.	25
Joseph, J. L.	100
Knapp, Shepherd	25
Laidlaw, John	100
Lawrence, Isaac	25
Leavitt, John W.	100
Lee, B. F.	100
Lenox, James	100
Leroy, Jacob R.	50
Lord, Rufus L.	100
Lorillard, Jacob	100
McIntyre, A.	100
Masters, Thomas	10
Michean, Henry	25
Michean, S.	10
Mihers, Henry	50
Milnor, Rev. Jas., D. D	200
Minturn, Rob. B.	200
Morris, Miss Charlotte	100
Murray, Misses	200
Nathan, S.	50
Nevins, Russel H.	200
Nevins, Rufus L.	100
Noble, John	200
Patten, Richard L.	100
Peet	20
Phelps, G. D.	10
Post, Gerardius	25
Prince, Edward.	200
Remson, Peter	200

Richards, Guy	$100
Roach, P. R.	100
Robinson, Morris	10
Rogers, George P.	100
Shipman, George P.	50
Stagg, John P. & Co	25
Stevens, Mrs. Dr.	100
St. Stephen's, member of	5
Stuyvesant, P. G.	400
Swan, Benjamin L.	100
Talbot, C. M.	200
Taylor, Jeremiah H.	50
Townsend, Elihu	100
Tracey, Frederick.	200
Van Wagener, H.	20
Varrick, Mrs. Maria.	100
Waldron, Mrs. Ann	10
Ward, Samuel	500
Warner, H. M	50
Watts, Mrs. Dr.	200
Whitlock, sen.	100
Whitlock, Samuel	200
Whitlock, S. B.	100
Whitney, Stephen	100
Wilder, S. V.	200
Willet, Mannius	200
Winston, F. S.	100
Woolley, B. L.	200

BOSTON.

Appleton, William	200
Armstrong, Sam'l. T.	50
Aspinwall	20
Baylies, E.	100
Borland, James	50
Bradford, Wm. B.	5
Cash	10
Caznove, Louis A.	50
Codman, Henry	200
Dunn, James C.	100
Edwards, Henry	100
Friend, by H. Upham	40
Grace Ch. Gent. and Wardens	200
Henshaw, Charles	50
Hind, E. S.	5
Holmes & Homer	30
Hubbard, S.	50
Hubbard, Wm. J.	50
Inskerman, Edward	100
Jeffries, John	100
Lambert, W. G.	20
Merrill, James C.	10
Newell, M.	50
Parker, Matthew L.	50
Parker, S. H.	5
Peters, Edward D.	100
Porter, Jonathan	50
Reynolds, Ed., Jr.	200
Reynolds, Wm. B.	100
Reynolds, Ladies at	100
Richardson, Benj. P.	10
Sargent, L. M	100

Shummin, William	$ 10	Cash	$ 5	
Snow, Gideon	20	Dawson, W. & Co.	100	
Stoddard, Charles	50	Donaldson, Johnson	10	
Stone, Jonas E.	100	Donnell, John	100	
Stone, Wm. B.	100	Dorsey, Richard	30	
Sullivan, William	20	Fisher, Charles	20	
Tappan, Charles	50	Gettings, John S.	100	
Tappan, John	200	Glenn, John	100	
Thayer, G. W.	10	Glenn, Mrs.	30	
Timmins, H	50	Glenn, Miss Jane	5	
Upham, Henry	100	Hoffman, Peter.	100	
Warren, J. C.	50	Hall, Professor.	25	
Weld, Aaron D.	50	Hanson, Mrs. H	30	
W. H.	50	Henderson, Andrew F.	10	
White, J. E.	20	J. G. D	20	
Willey, N.	20	Jones, Talbot	50	
Winthrop, Thomas S.	100	Krebbs, William	20	
		Kurl, Mr	10	

PROVIDENCE.

		Legg, Miss	1	
Adams, Joseph	3	McKimm, Isaac	100	
Adams, Seth, jr	10	Morris, J. B.	50	
Allen, Miss Candace	25	Nelson, Robert	20	
Allen, Mrs. Harriet	20	Reed, John	15	
Aplin, William	5	Riggs, Samuel	20	
Barton, Henry	5	Scott, Miss	1	
Burgess, Thomas	20	Shoemaker, Mr.	5	
Butler, Cyrus	20	St. Peter's Lecture Room, at	8	
Cash	35 38	Thompson, Henry	20	
Chace, John B.	5	Toothunter, Joseph	50	
Cheney, Charles	10	Whiteford, Dr	10	
Dorr, Sullivan	10	Woodward, Mr.	20	
Dyer, Charles, jr	5			
Farnum, John	5			
Goddard, Mr.	5			
Goff, Dr.	5	**PHILADELPHIA.**		
Grace Church Collection	50	Ashurst, L. R.	100	
Griscom, J.	5	Ashurst, Richard	100	
Guinett, G.	1	Cash	30	
Ides, J. A.	10	Delancy, W. H.	50	
Ives, Robert H.	20	Dundas, James	20	
Ives, Thomas P.	100	Elnas, Thomas	100	
Jenkins, William	20	Farr, John	50	
Jones, Alexander	10	Gommez, Mrs.	20	
Manton, Amasa	40	Ingersol, C.	30	
Miller, L. L.	10	Lex, Jacob	100	
Taylor, John	10	Mitchell, Dr. K.	100	
Thayer, William	5	Mitchell, T.	100	
Wardwell, G. S.	5	Musgrave, William	20	
Waterman, R.	25	Pratt, Henry	20	
Widow	1	Reed, John	15	
		Robins, Thomas	10	
		Stevenson, Cornelius	100	
BALTIMORE.		Stott, Mrs. Elizabeth	200	
Albert, Jacob	50	St. Paul's, Cash	51 50	
Anderson, F.	100	Tilghman, Mrs.	5	
Boyle, II.	100	Vanderkemp, H.	50	
Baltzell, A.	10	Wagner, Tobias	100	
Baltzell, Charles	20	Watson, Charles C.	50	
Bradford, Miss', School	8	White, Bishop	50	
Brown, H	100			
Cash	10	**BROOKLYN.**		
Cash	20	Anderson, David J	10	
Cash	10	Brush, Conklin	100	
		Back, Judah	20	

Back. Robert	$200	Onderdonk, Mrs	$ 10
Betts, William	25	Peet, Frederick T	200
Brown, Rodman & Samuel	50	Perry, J. A	50
Buckley, J. W	2	Pettit, Robert	20
Cash	5	Pierpont, Mary (Mite Society	
Carter, Robert	200	for Kenyon)	7
Chapin, John	50	Rapellye, Jacob	200
Chew, J. L	100	Reed, Philip	100
Child, Asa	5	Richard, Charles H	100
Clarke, James H	100	Ripley, George B	2
Clarkson, Matthew	200	Ripley, W. D	2
Congdon, Charles, for Sabbath-		Robinson, Thomas	5
school Teachers	50	Rockwell, Charles W	200
Cornell, W. J	50	Rockwell, J. A	10
Dean, William R	10	Sands, Joseph	200
Denton, Nehemiah	50	Sands, Mrs. (charity box)	6 12
Donsey, L	20	Small sums collected	230 50
Doughty, John S	20	St. Ann's Education Society	200
Embury, Mr	50	St. Ann's Monthly Collection,	32 88
Flagler, P	100	Swift, David D	100
Gamble, John M	100	Tucker, F. C	200
Gilmer, William C	10	Tucker, Thatcher	200
Goddard, Calvin	20	Tyler, Mrs Calvin	2
Graham, John B	100	Vansinderns, Mr. (at)	100
Green, William P	100	Webster, Horace	100
Green, Mrs. William P	20	Williams, Edward	25
Green, E. H	1	Williams, Erastus	10
Green, Mrs	1	Williams, H. C	1
Hibbard, Andrews	20	Willoughby, Samuel A	50
Howland, G. S	50		
Hoyt, Charles	1000	NEW LONDON.	
Huntington, G	10	Allyn, Francis	10
Johnson, Rev. E	100	Cash	1 50
Jones, G. A	1	Cash	28 85
Kenney, J. W	1	Cleaveland, Sophia	1
Kissam, Joseph	100	Frink, A	2
Luquier, Nicholas	100	Hallam, Rev. Edward	100
Lathrop, D., jr	2	Hurlbutt, Joseph	50
Lawman, R	2	Lady (from a)	5
Lee, Alfred	100	Williams, Thomas B	50
Lee, Mrs. E	100	Wilson, Increase	3
Napier, John	50	Woodbridge, Miss	10
Newman, Alexander	10		

MISCELLANEOUS.

Congregation, Collection	$181	Lancaster, Pa.
Cutler Samuel	50	Portland, Maine.
Davies, Professor	50	West Point.
Delevan, Henry W	200	Ballston.
Gardner, Capt. J. L	20	Fort Hamilton.
Greenleaf, Mr	10	Cambridge, Mass.
Johnson, Rev. R	50	Hyde Park, N. Y.
Lady	1	Troy, N. Y.
Lambard, A	10	Augusta, Maine.
McIlvaine, Joseph	2	Gambier, Ohio.
Minor, Mrs. Lucy L	40	Fredericksburg, Virginia.
Muhlenburgh, Rev. Mr	100	Flushing, L. I.

Newton. E. N.........................$200 ....Pittsfield, Mass.
Sands, Mr. Thomas..... .... 50 ....Liverpool, England.
Smith, Miss............................ 20 ....New Brunswick.
Van Rensselaer, Gen................ 200 ....Albany.
Warren, Nathan...................... 200 ....Troy,
Warren, Stephen..................... 200 ....Troy.
Wallace, John B....................... 50 ....Meadville, Pa.

In all the above is $26,600.

A TEMPORARY PROFESSORSHIP IN THE THEOLOGICAL SEMINARY.

While the preceding collections were in progress, another important object was accomplished, mainly in New York and Brooklyn: viz., to provide for a five year's Professorship in the Theological Seminary. It was by this means that, in connection with the Milnor Professorship, the organization of the Theological Seminary was first completed. Till now the Rev. Dr. Sparrow, sustained in part by the Milnor Professorship, devoted his time mainly to academical instruction. In 1833, however, classes were organized in the Seminary, and regular recitations begun. The Rev. Dr. Sparrow being Milnor Professor of Systematic Divinity, and the Rev. Dr. Muenscher Professor of Biblical Literature.

The following is from the subscription list, on which $1,220 is marked paid:

BROOKLYN.

Chew, Thomas J................ $40
Clarke, Mrs. J. H.............. 40
Cooper, William................ 40
Graham, J. B.................... 40
Hallam, Mr. N., New London, by Mr. Chew, Brooklyn.. 40
Hoyt, Charles.................... 40
Peet, Frederick T.............. 40
Pierpont, Misses, and Mrs. R. S. Tucker.................... 30
Sands, Joseph................... 40
St. Ann's ten Female Teachers, by Miss Sarah White... 40
St. Ann's Male Teachers, by Richard L. White..... 40
Tucker, R. S. and Wm. Carter, 40
Tucker, Thatcher............... 40

NEW YORK CITY.

Burtus, James A................ 40
Dominick, Mr. James W...... 40

Dominick, Miss Ann........... $20
Eastburn, Rev. Manton, D. D. 40
Gillett, Horatio and John Moore 30
Gitteau, Abner L............... 20
Hoyt, James J.................. 40
Milnor, Rev. James, D. D...... 40
Rutgers, Col. Nicholas G....... 40
Routch, Peter R. and E. W. Waldgrave 10
Shatzell, Mr..................... 10
Tracey, Frederick A............ 100
Watts, Mrs. John............... 40
Whitlock, William, jr.......... 40
Willett, Dr. Mannius.......... 40
Willett, Mrs., his mother...... 40
Winston, Frederick S 40
Woolley, Mr..................... 40

COLUMBUS, OHIO.

Wilcox, P. B., Esq.............. 40
                              _____
                              $1,220 00

SUBSCRIPTION FOR BUILDING A HOUSE, AT GAMBIER, FOR THE BISHOP OF THE DIOCESE.

At Bishop Chase's settlement with the Trustees, in 1829, the sum of $3,037 was found to be due to him. Of this sum he gave $2,000 to the Institution, $1,000 of which was on condition that it be applied toward building a house for the Bishop of the Diocese, upon a site to be designated by himself. The site was not designated, and the building not erected.

Upon the consecration of Bishop McIlvaine, an unsuccessful effort was made in the diocese to raise funds for this purpose, and although only the following sums were obtained, a house was erected for the Bishop, by the Institution :

H. B. Curtis, Esq..............	$ 5	Cincinnati	$150
Rev. J. O'Brien...............	20	J. Johnston, jr................	3
Kellogg & Allen, Cleveland...	50	Robert Johnston..............	5
Cash, Columbus...............	120	Col. Brush, Chillicothe......	10
Rev. W. N. Lyster............	25	Barber and others, Ohio City,	38
By Rev. Mr. Preston..........	130		
Rev. James McElroy...........	33		$609 00
Ashtabula....................	20		

COLLECTION IN OHIO BY REV. DR. SPARROW, IN 1839.

It is well known that buildings commonly cost more than is anticipated. So it was at Gambier. When the buildings were completed, for which funds had been solicited in 1833, there was a debt of some $16,000, and there seemed no way to meet it, unless the Church in Ohio could be persuaded to do its share of the work. This, the Trustees determined to attempt. The Rev. Dr. Sparrow was requested to undertake the agency; and, considering the pecuniary depression of the times, and the partial application made, the effort was successful.

The whole sum subscribed was $7,348 82, of which $605 25 was cash, and the balance in notes of hand, which have been paid only in part, and some after years of delay.

The names of those prompt men who paid cash are not now to be found. The following is an account of the notes, so far as they appear to have been paid :

Adams, Daniel,...............	$100	Andrews, J. W.............	50
Avery, Alfred................	50	Baldwin, Joseph............	50
Alexander, A. C..............	25	Buttles, Joel, balance........	32

Middleton, Strobridge & Co. Litho. Cin. O.

BEXLEY HALL.

Buttles, A..	$50	Orr, Thomas	$50
Clements, John.	25	Owen, George	25
Crane, J. H	50	Peet, Rev. Mr	100
Creighton, Hon.	50	Pinney, A. H	150
Crouse	40	Reed, Mrs	250
Doane, G. W	50	Ridgeway, J. jr	50
Doddridge, J..P. and B	250	Rose, Levi	25
Dyer, Rev. H.	100	Sanford, Rev. A	25
Edwards, D	50	Sawyer, Noah	100
Ely, Mr	20	Schenck, R. C	25
French, Jeremiah	15	Sill, J.	20
French, Mansfield	25	Smallwood, Rev. W. A	20
Gilbert, J. W	50	Smith, Prof. R. P...	250
Griffin, Apollos	10	Swearingen, Col	50
Hazlett, Robert	50	Thatcher. N. W	50
Hall, G. A	50	Thomas, Jesse B	100
Hayden, P.	50	Varian, Edward	20
Huffnagle, Mr	25	Wallace, Mr	50
Irvine, W. W	93 82	Watts, Dr	50
Keck, George	50	Whiting, I. N	300
Mansfield, J	20	Wilcox, Mr	30
Mitchel, M. H	50	Wing, Rev. M. T. C	500
Minor, J. L	50	Wood, Mr..	100
Matthews, D	50	Woodbridge, J	100
Monger, Warren	25	Woodbury, P.	50
Norton, D. S	500		
Neil, W	100	Total	$5,341 82

A Second Effusion of English Benevolence.

In the year 1835, Bishop McIlvaine made a visit to England; and, as was quite natural when there, sought the society of those clergy of the English Church with whom he more particularly sympathized. It was the practice, at that time, of some of the London clergy, to the number of about one hundred, to meet stately at Islington, for the purpose of clerical conference and communion, and for social prayer. Rev. Daniel Wilson, then recently made Bishop of Calcutta, and the Rev. Thomas Hartwell Horne, were among the number.

To this meeting Bishop McIlvaine was invited; and when there, was asked to give an account of the condition and prospects of religion in his own country and Diocese. In doing so, our Bishop spoke of the " vastly greater increase of population than of clergy; and how many of the inhabitants of those destitute regions are emigrants from England, accustomed once to the green pastures of our parent Church." After alluding to the tide of immigration by which this wonderful growth has been effected, as still flowing and still swelling, and stating that such is the extent of new land to be occupied, and such the fertility of the soil in general, that population may continue for a long time to flow on at its present ratio of increase, without a check from deficiency of room, or of maintenance. He urged it as an interesting and affecting consideration to Christians of Great Britain, that a very large part of this living stream is directly from among themselves. "Not only is the Popery of those regions transplanted, in a great measure, by settlers from the United Kingdom, but among the hundreds of thousands for whom the ministry is to be supplied, * * Protestant Englishmen and Protestant Irishmen, with their families, are every-where seen, sometimes in colonies almost by themselves, at other times mixed up with people from other countries; but every-where entreating him most earnestly to send them the ministry, with the ordinances to which they were once accustomed." This was listened to by the assembled clergy with profound attention.

Then the Lord Bishop of Calcutta asked our Bishop what he would have them do, or rather what they could do for him and his Diocese? Though our Bishop had not intended to appeal to the liberality of the British public, yet when thus generously pressed, he suggested the need of a building expressly for theological students.

Accordingly, a plan, with minute working drafts and a papier maché model, was gotten up by Mr. Henry Roberts, a London Architect; after which plan Baxley Hall has been erected at Gambier, with funds obtained chiefly in England; a building, the beauty of which has not been surpassed by any of like dimensions in Ohio.

The following are the names of contributors:

HER ROYAL HIGHNESS THE DUCHESS OF KENT.................. £10
HER ROYAL HIGHNESS THE DUCHESS OF GLOUCESTER............ 10
HER ROYAL HIGHNESS THE PRINCESS AUGUSTA................. 10
THE DUCHESS OF BEAUFORT................................. 5
Right Rev. the LORD BISHOP OF LONDON 20
Right Rev. the LORD BISHOP OF WINCHESTER............... 10
Right Rev. the LORD BISHOP OF SALISBURY................ 10
Right Rev. the LORD BISHOP OF LITCHFIELD AND COVENTRY.. 5
Right Rev. the LORD BISHOP OF CALCUTTA................. 60
Right Hon. the EARL OF CARNARVON....................... 10
Right Hon. LORD BEXLEY................................. 50
Right Hon. LORD DARTMOUTH.............................. 10
Right Hon. LORD MOUNTSANFORD........................... 10
Right Hon. LORD TEIGNMOUTH............................. 5
Right Hon. LORD KENYON................................. 20

A. B. C. .... £1 1 | Acland, Mrs. C., per Mrs.
A. B. C. .... 10 | Jenkinson £1
Acland, Sir Thomas.... 25 | Acland, A., Esq., by same..... 1 1

Name	£	s
Adye, Colonel	£1	
A. G. J.	2	
Agnew, Sir Andrew	3	3
Agnew, Miss M.	1	
Anderson, Rev. J., Brighton.	1	
Anderson, Rev. R. "	1	
Andover, Lady, per Mrs. Jenkinson		10
Anonymous	10	
Anonymous	10	
Anonymous	11	12
Anonymous	1	12
Anonymous	3	3
Anonymous, in Dr. Mayo's drawing-room	3	3
Anonymous, by Miss Hoare..	2	2
Anonymous, found among the books		15
Anonymous, per T. W. West, Esq., Mag. Hall, Ox		10
Arnauld, J. M. D	5	5
Anonymous	50	
Auncial, Rev. Edward	1	
Auncial, Miss		10
Austey, G. S., Esq., St. Alban's Hall		10
Baker, Rev. R. G	5	
Ball, J., St. John's, Oxford....	1	1
Baring, Sir Thomas	20	
Barnes, Mrs. John	5	
Baronneau, Mrs.	2	
Barrington, Hon. and Rev....	5	
Barrington, Lady	10	
Bates, Joshua, Esq	50	
Battersby, Harford, Esq	10	
Baxter, N., Esq	1	
Beardmore, Miss	5	
Bell, Capt		10
Bentley, James, Esq	5	
Bevan, Robert, Esq	2	
Bevan, Rev. W	10	
Bird, Rev. C. S	10	
Blandy, Rev. Mr.	1	
B., Lady	3	
Bocket, D., Esq., Hemstead, per L. B. Seeley & Sons...	2	
Bloomfield, Sir T	5	
Bodley, Dr., Hull	1	1
Brodie, Lady, £5, Brodie, Miss, 3s	5	3
Brandram, Rev. A	5	
Brewer, John Watson, Derby	1	
Brien, Hon. Mrs.	1	
Brien, J. O	1	
Bridges, J., Esq	10	
Bridges, Rev. Nathaniel	10	
Bridges, Rev. Charles	11	10
Broderick, C., Esq	23	
Brooke, S. B., Esq	5	
Brown, Rev. Thomas, Christ Hospital	2	
Buchen, Geo., Esq., Nettow..	5	
Buckley, Rev. H. W	£1	1
Buller, Lady, per Mrs. Jenkinson	1	
Burroughs, Lieut. G	1	10
Burrows, Lieut. A		10
Burt, Capt	1	
Butler, Mr. E	1	
Cattley, John, Esq	5	
Campbell, Rev. Colin.	1	
Cambridge	44	4
Cardwell, Principal, St. Alban's Hall, and Prof. Ancient History, Oxford	2	
Carter, Miss.	1	
Carter, Miss M.	1	
Carver, Rev. J., Islington	1	
Carver, Mrs. "	1	
Caswell, Rev. R. C., Wilts....	5	
Chalmers, E., per F. Sandys, Esq.	1	
Chambers, R., Esq	10	
Champneys, Rev. W. W., Brazen Nose	1	
Chapman, Wm., Esq., Newcastle.	5	
Chatterton, Sir William	2	
Chatterton, Lady	1	
Charlesworth, Mr., High Harrowgate		10
Chester, Dean of	3	
C. H. & E., by Rev. R. Hayne, Henlow	30	
Childers, M. W., Brighton....	2	
Childers, Hon. Mrs.	5	
Cholmely, Miss S	1	1
Chalmondely, Marg.	10	
Clark, Rev. Henry, Harnston Lodge	2	
Claypon, Bartholomew, Esq., Hempstead	1	
Claypon, Joshua, Hempstead.	1	
Clayton, Rev. G	5	
Close, Samuel, Hust	1	1
Clowes, Rev. Thomas, Great Yarmouth	6	16
Cobb, Rev. W. T		10
Cook, James, Esq.	25	
Cordes, J. J	10	
Courtney, W. R., Esq		10
Couskney, Rev. Mr.	1	1
Cox, S. C., Esq	5	
Cox, Miss.	1	
Creswell, Miss.	1	
Crewe, Misses	3	
Cunningham, Rev. J. W	2	
Cunningham, W., Esq	5	
Cunningham, Rev. F.	3	
Dalley, Mrs.	1	
Day, Rev. Rob., Rector, Sunderland	5	
Darley, Rev. J.	1	
Davis, Rev. John, Worcester..	5	

Name	£	s
Dawes, Thomas, Esq............	£10	
Dealtry, Rev. Dr.........	5	
Dent, Miss, per Mrs. Jenkinson	2	
Deverill, Mrs. Eliza...........	5	
Devisine, Rev. L., Brighton...	10	
Disney, Mrs. Wm., Somerset, near Black Rock, Dublin...	2	
Dixon, William, Esq., Blackheath	10	
Dodsworth, Mr., per Mrs. Jenkinson............	1	1
Dodsworth, Mrs...............	1	
Donaldson, Mrs., per Mrs. Jenkinson	1	
Douglas, Rev. P. M............	2	
Dyne, Rev. J., Edmonton ...	1	1
Elkins, Mrs., Brighton.........	1	
Elliott, Mrs., Westfield Lodge, Brighton	2	
Elliott, Rev. H. V., Brighton	2	
Emigrant well-wisher.........	50	
Estcourt, Rev. E., collected by.........	1	2
Evelyn, Mrs.....................	1	1
Ewbank, Henry.................	25	
Fancourt, Rev. T.........		5
Fanshaw, Capt	1	
Farley, Rev. Thomas...........	1	1
Fenn, Rev. J., collected by ..	27	18
Fern, Rev. Joseph............	5	
Fielden, Mrs.....................	1	
Finmore, Lieut.................		10
Fisher, Rev. R. D., Basildon	2	
Fletcher, Capt. E. C............	1	
Fletcher, Miss L................	3	
Floyer, J., Esq.................	1	
Forbes, Miss....................	5	
Forster, Miss, Southend......	2	2
Foyster, Rev. H S............	5	
Fox, Mr., Durham...............	5	
Fox, Mrs., "	2	
Fox, Miss, "	1	
Fox, Miss Ann, "	1	
Fox, Rev. John.................	1	
Frazer, Lady....................	1	
Frazer, Sir A....................	1	
Frazer, Lieut. H................	1	
Frere, Jas. H., Esq............	2	
Friends, eight..................	36	14
Friends, per D. Ruell.........	5	
Friend, by Rev. T. Tyndale, Holton	10	
Friend, young..................		3
Friends, three, by Dr. MacBride..........................	3	
Friends, by Miss Simmonds		10
Friends, three, Brighton......	12	
Friends, two, by Mrs. Jenks, Brighton	2	
Friends...........................	19	5
Friend, by Rev. Mr. Yate......	1	1
Friends two, by Rev. Dr. Rumsey	£ 2	
Gadsden, James, Esq., Hull...	10	
Garrett, W. A., Esq., Hampsted..	5	
Gay, Geo., Esq.................	10	
Gentleman..................	1	
Gladstone, W., Esq., M. P....	5	
Gilliot, John, Esq.............	10	
Graham, T. H., Esq., Edmund Castle............	2	
Grant, Lieut............		10
Gray, W. Esq., York...........	5	
Gray, Mrs. Walker, Brunswick, Esq., Brighton.........	2	
Greaves, John, Esq............	1	
Greaves, Henry, Esq.........	1	
Greaves, Miss....................	1	
Gregory, Dr.....................	2	
Gregory, Miss Annie		10
Gregory, Mr. C. H............		10
Grenfell, P. H. Leger, Esq...	10	
Grey, Sir G., Bart., per Mrs. Jenkinson	2	
Grimshawe, Rev. T. J., Biddenham.........	5	
Grinton, Miss...................	1	
Goode, Rev. F., per.........	15	
Goode, Rev. Francis...........	5	
Gower, Edwin, Esq.............	10	10
Gutterage, Joshua, Esq., Denmark Hill.........	5	
H., Mr.........................	5	
Hall, Rev. J.....................	1	
Hall, Miss, Bourton on the Wakes, Gloucestershire...	2	
Halliday, Mrs........		10
Hambleton, Rev. J., Islington, per F. Sandys, Esq.........	1	
Hambleton, G., Esq............	2	
Hamilton, Maj	1	1
Hamilton, Lady.................	1	
Hancock, Rev. W., Minister, Kilburn.........	1	
Hancock, Samuel, Esq., per do	1	
Hanford, Rev. A	2	
Hankey, Wm. Alers	5	5
Hankey, T., Esq...............	5	
Hardcastle, Joseph, Esq......	10	
Hardcastle, Miss............	10	
Harding, Rev. John, per—— Chelsea............	10	
Hartop, Lady, per Mrs. Jenkinson	10	
Hardinge, Mrs..................	1	
Hart, G. B., Esq., Newington	5	
Hardy, John, Esq., M. P......	5	
Harwood, Rev. John.........	1	
Haseltine, W., Esq......... ...	5	
Hatchard, Mrs., and son......	2	
Hawker, Capt. R. N............	3	

Name	£	s
Hawkins, Rev. Dr., Provost, Oriel Coll., Oxford	3	3
Hawkesworth, Mrs		10
Hayne, Rev. W. B	2	
Hewitson, H., Esq., New Castle Tyne	1	
Hewitson, Mrs	1	
H. E. B	1	1
H. H., from Mrs. Nisbet	1	1
Hibbert, Miss Catherine	1	1
Hibbert, Miss Sarah	1	1
Hibbert, Mr. John	1	1
Hibbert, Edward	1	1
Hibbert, Miss	1	1
Hill, J., St. Edmund's Hall, Oxford	1	17
Hitchings, Mrs., Wargrove	1	1
Handman, Josiah, Esq., Walthamstow		10
Hoare. H., Esq., per Mrs. Jenkinson	10	11
Hoare, Wm., Esq	1	1
Hoare, G. N., Esq	1	
Hoare, Mrs. Hugh	1	
Hoare, Miss	1	
Hoare, Miss, Grosvenor Sqr.		15
Holton, Rev. J, Tyndale	2	
Hope, Capt., Brighton	1	
Hope, Lady	1	
Hope, Miss, Brighton	2	
Hope, Miss	1	
Horne, Rev. T., Hartwell	2	
Howard, Rev. T	2	
Hudson, W. B., Haymarket	5	
Hulme, Rev. George	10	
Hunter, Sir Claudius	5	
Hulton, Rev. T. P	1	1
Inglis, Lady	1	
Inglis, S. R. H., Bart	10	
Inglis, Miss	1	
Irvine, Miss	10	
Jackson, Henry, Esq., Tutbury	1	15
Jackson, Henry, Esq., Tutbury, by him	3	5
Jawbron, Magdalen Hall, Oxford	2	2
Jenkinson, Capt., per	10	
Jerram, Rev. Mr	10	
Johnstone, Lady	1	
Johnstone, Miss		10
Jowett, Rev. H., per	2	1
J. W	1	
Kemble, Edward, Esq	50	
Kemble, Henry, Esq	50	
Kennan, Miss	1	
Kennedy, Rev. B. N	5	
Kenshaw, Mr., per F. Sandys, Esq	1	
Key, H. C., Esq	1	1
Killey, Esq		10
Kingston, Mrs. & Miss, Br't'n.	2	
Knight, Rev. George	1	1
L., Miss	1	
L., Mr. J		10
Labouchere, John, Esq	10	
Ladies, four	4	2
Lally, Mrs. Edmund, High Harrowgate	1	
Lally, Misses, High Harrowgate		10
Lane, Mr. and Mrs., Brighton	2	
Langston, Rev. S., by Shef'd	5	
Lawrence, Joseph, Esq	5	
Leather, P. H., Esq	1	
Leger, P. H. Greenfell	10	
Lemon, Miss	1	
Lettsom, W. Manson, Esq	1	
Lewis, Rev. R. G., Streatham, Surrey	2	
Lindsey, Capt		10
Linton, Rev. H	1	1
Little boy in Dorsetshire, collected by	4	
Livingston, Rev., by himself and others	19	5
Lodge, Mrs., of Carlisle	1	1
Long, W., Esq., by	10	
Longley, Rev. Dr., Harrow	5	
Longmore, Mr	1	
Lourdan, Miss E., Horsham	1	
Lucas, Dr		10
Macbride, Dr., Prin. Mag. Hall, Oxford	2	
McClintock, Mrs	1	
Mackworth, Maj., and friends	10	
MacLean, Mrs	1	
MacLean, Miss		10
MacLean, Miss A		10
Mac T., W	1	
Mac Taggart, Mrs	5	
M. A. H., by Dr. Dealtry	5	
Maitland, Fuller, Esq.	5	
Maitland, Miss	1	
Maitland, Miss F.	5	
Maitland, Miss B. F.	5	
Maitland, Miss Anna	1	
Maitland, Rev. L. D., Brighton	1	11
Manfield, W., Esq	5	
Manners, Capt.		10
Mapleton, Rev. Mr	1	
Marriatt, Charles, M. A., Fellow of Oriel	10	
Marsh, Rev. E. G., Hempstead, per Seeley and sons	1	
Mayo, Rev. Dr	2	
Mayo, Mrs. C	1	
Mayo, Miss	1	
Meeting at Brighton, collected at	26	
Member of Jews' Chapel, by the minister	5	
Michell, William, Esq	5	

Name	£	s.
Miller, Boyd, Esq	5	
Mithurn, Rev. T. H	2	2
M. M.	5	
Molyneaux, Rev. C	1	
Monro, Rev. R	1	1
Monro, Mrs. A		10
Moore, Miss Catherine	1	
Moore, R. W., per F. Sandys, Esq		10
Moore, Rev. Robert	1	1
Mortimer, Rev. T., Islington	1	1
Moseley, Sir Oswald	10	10
Mrs. ——	1	
Mondrell, Miss		10
Nach, Esq		5
Natt, Rev. S., Vicar of St. Sepulcher	50	
Neville, Rev. H	5	
Neville, Miss	1	
Nicolls, Col	1	
Noel, Hon., and Rev. T	1	1
Noel, Hon., and Rev. J	5	
Noel, Rev. Baptist W	5	
Northcote, Esq	2	2
N. and S., Misses, by Rev. W. R. Hayne, Henlow	5	10
Oldfield, Esq	2	
Orgar, Rev. W	2	2
Orgar, Pupils of		16
Oxman, Rev. W	1	
Paine, Rev. Wm., Yarmouth	2	
Palmer, Archdale, Esq	5	
Palmer, Mrs.	1	
Parker, Mrs., Guernsey	1	1
Parsons, Mrs. J., by Mrs. Reay	1	
Payne, J. R., Sec. Bible Soc. Tower, collected by	15	1
Payne, Cornelius, Esq., Hemstead	5	
Paynter, John, Esq	5	5
Penny donations		5
Percy, Rev. W	2	2
Phipps, Hon., & Rev. Augustus	10	
Pifford, Mr., per F. Sandys, Esq	1	
Plumptree, Rev. J	10	
Poinder, John, Esq	10	
Poole, R., Esq	5	
Porcher, Charles, Esq	3	
Pott, Mrs. Charles	2	
Pownal, H., Esq	10	10
Pownal, Mrs. Amelia	5	
Praid, Esq., per Mrs. Jenkinson	5	
Pratt, Rev. Josiah, & friends	5	
Pratt, Rev. J. S	10	
Prest, Mrs., York	2	
Preston, Rev. N.N., Cheshunt Vicarage	5	
Prince, R., per F. Sandys, Esq.	1	1

Name	£	s.
Pusey, Lady E	5	
Pusey, P., Esq	5	
Purvis, Henry, Esq	10	
Ramsey, D., Esq	5	
Ranking, John, Esq	2	
Ravensworth, Lady	5	
Reay, Rev. S., St. Alban's Hall	1	
Record, Newspaper	107	4
Redfearn, Mrs	5	
Ridley, Mrs. H. C., Oxford	5	
Rivers, Miss		10
Robins, Mr., one of his congregation	5	
Roberts, H., Esq	2	
Roberts, C., Esq	3	3
Roberts, Isaiah, Esq	5	
Robertson, Capt	1	
Robinson, Rev. Sir John	20	
Roe, Rev. Peter	20	
Ronson, William, Esq., Carlisle	5	
Ruell, D., per	5	
Rumsey, N., Esq., Beaconsfield	5	
Rumsey, Rev. Dr	5	
Russell, Rev. W	1	
Rusticius		10
Sale, Rev. T., Southgate	1	1
Sale, Mrs	1	1
Sally, Misses, 10s., Sally, Mrs. Edmund, £1	1	10
Salmond, Col	1	
Sanders, Rev. J., collected by	6	
Saunders, Rev. Robert	5	
Sawyer, Wm., Esq	5	
Scott, Mrs., widow's mite	1	
Scott, Major, H. A	1	
Schneider, Miss	1	
Seymore, Lady	1	1
Servants at H. Hoare's, Esq.		11
Shaw, Lady	10	
Sharp, Mr	1	
Shepherd, Rev. John	1	
Shirley, Rev. W	1	
Shuttleworth, Rev. Dr., Warden New College, Oxford	2	
S., Miss	1	
Small sums, by Mrs. Jenkinson	4	18
Small sums, per Mrs. R. Baxter, Doncaster		10
Smith, Rev. J. Pye, D.D	2	8
Smith, Mr. Robert	2	
Smith, Miss C. C		10
Smith, Mr. L		5
Snell, Rev. Mr	10	
Snow, Rev. W., collected by	10	
Snow, Mrs	1	
Somerset, Lady Mary	1	
Stamforth, Rev. F. J	10	
Stankoff, Dr	1	

	£	s.
Stapleton, Rev. Mr., per Mrs. Jenkinson	£1	
Stewart, H. G. K.	2	
Strachan, J. M., Esq.	5	
Stranger	2	
Student, Trin. Coll., Dublin..	1	
Stone, William, Esq., Denmark Hill	5	
Sperling, Miss H., Brighton..	1	
Sperling, Miss, "	1	1
Spurling, Mr., Islington	1	
Sutterly, Rev. W. L.	1	
S. W.	1	
Tait, J. C., Esq	1	
Terry, Avison, Esq., Hull	3	
Terry, John, Esq.	2	
Thompson, Mrs., of Sheldon Lodge, collection and donation	10	10
Thornton, Henry, Esq	20	
Tiddesmau, Rev. Mr., by Mrs. Symmouds		10
Tidden, Mrs.	1	
Trevor, George, Esq., Oxford, per	77	5
Troche, Rev. T., Brighton		10
Trueman, Joseph, Esq.	10	
Twells, Mr., per F. Sandys, Esq.	1	
Valpy, Rev. Dr., Reading	2	2
Vansittart, Mrs.	10	
Vivian, Mr., Edinburgh	5	
Wake, Miss, Brighton	5	
Walker, Thomas, Esq., Denmark Hill	10	
Wall, William, Esq.	5	
Wall, Mrs.	1	
Waldgrave, Hon. Harriet	5	13
Watkins, Rev. H. G., Rector St. Swithin's	2	
Warwick, W. J., Esq.	10	
Webb, Miss		10
Webb, Sir John	2	2
Webb, Lady	1	1
West, Miss, Brighton	1	

	£	s.
West, Mrs., Brighton.	£1	
West, T. W., Mag. Hall, Oxford, by		10
Weston, Mrs	1	1
Wetherby, Mr. F.		10
Wetherby, Mrs. Richard	1	
Wetherby, Miss S.	1	
Weylan, John, Esq.	10	
Whitmore, John, Esq.	5	
Whitmore, Mrs., per Mrs. Jenkinson	1	
White, Mrs. William, per Mrs. Reay	5	
Wiggin, Timothy, Esq.	240	
Williams & Co., by	28	6
Williams & Co., from Winchester	70	7
Widow's mite		10
Wilks, Charles	2	
Williams, Robert	10	
Williams, Mrs.	5	
Williams, Robert, Jr., Esq...	5	
Williams, Miss	2	
Wilmot, Sir R., Brighton	1	1
Wilson, Rev. Daniel	5	
Wilson, Joseph, Esq., Brighton	10	
Wilson, Rev. Carus, Cambridge	15	16
Wolfe, Baron, per Mrs. Jenkinson	3	
Wood, Basil George, Esq.	2	2
Woodroffe, Rev. T., Colburn, Isle of Wight	2	10
Y., Mrs		5
Yard, Rev., Brighton		10
Yeatman, F., Esq	3	
Young, Miss Florence	1	1
Young Gentlemen of Cheam School	2	13
The sum of the above if correctly copied, should be £2,918	13	
Net, $12,370 07.		

N. B.—The name of the one through whom a donation is made, is not in all cases put down, and small sums, anonymous, have, in some cases, been grouped together.

The reader will notice with pleasure how much of the collecting for benevolent objects is done in England by voluntary agents, occupying prominent positions in society.

In addition to the above, Bishop McIlvaine, in his address to the Convention, in 1835, mentioned the receipt of 1,902 volumes for the Library, from friends in England. The venerable Mrs. Hannah More, at the close of life, remembered Ohio, and bequeathed to Sir Thomas Acland £200, in trust for its Bishop; the particular object to be designated by her executor. It was designated as the foundation for a scholarship in the Theological Seminary, the interest being always applicable to the support of a student in that department.

This visit of Bishop McIlvaine resulted in the following pleasing interchange of sentiment between the members of the English Universities and those of our own Seminary and College:

To THE RIGHT REVEREND CHARLES P. McILVAINE, D. D., BISHOP OF OHIO, AND PRESIDENT OF KENYON COLLEGE, IN THE UNITED STATES OF AMERICA.

Right Reverend Sir—The undersigned, Bachelors and Undergraduates of the University of Oxford, have learned with cordial sympathy the objects of your mission to this country.

Ourselves participators in the blessings of an University, founded by the liberality and piety of our common ancestors, we can not but take a deep interest in the progress of an institution which, under circumstances of greater difficulty, is entering in a distant land on the same course of religious and useful learning.

Nor is it forgotten by us, that Kenyon College, no less than our own venerable University, is intimately connected with the Protestant Episcopal Church. We rejoice to know, that its religious instruction is superintended by a Branch of the Church of Christ, which we esteem it a privilege to greet as the daughter of our Apostolical Establishment. And we reflect with the kindest feelings of Christian fellowship, that in one faith, one language, and one form of expression, our brother Students in Ohio and ourselves daily worship the God of our Fathers.

With such sentiments we are anxious to offer to you, sir, and the members of Kenyon College, the assurance of a sympathy, which we trust will not be unacceptable to them, by contributing toward the erection of the proposed Theological College.

In requesting you to be the channel through which we may convey these feelings, we desire to join with them an expression of the regret and esteem with which we regard your own character as a Theologian and a Christian Bishop. Earnestly do we pray, that it may please God to give you a prosperous journey to your native land; and long to preserve the blessings of your oversight to His Church, where amid the increasing labors of your Diocese, and the arduous struggle that is prepared for the Members of the College over which you preside, we venture to hope that You and They will sometimes remember with pleasure, that "we have wished you good luck, ye that are of the House of the Lord."

We have the honor to remain, Right Reverend Sir, with every sentiment of esteem and respect, your attached and faithful Servants.

Signed,   GEORGE TREVOR, *S. C. L. Magdalen Hall*,

        J. E. GILES, *Lusby Scholar*,   "   "

        WILLIAM BEADOW HEATHCOTE, *S. C. L. New College,*

And two hundred and eighty-six others, Members and Undergraduates of eighteen different Colleges.

—

TRINITY COLLEGE, Cambridge, May 25, 1835.

My Dear Friend—On your leaving England to return to your arduous duties in Ohio, there are many here who wish to express to you the deep interest they feel in your welfare, and in the prosperity of your College and Diocese. We desire particularly to cherish the feelings of our entire oneness with those churches in the United States, which the Lord has intrusted to your oversight; and we would assure them, through you, of our affectionate sympathy and regard. We are attached to them, not merely as Christians who love and serve the same Lord and Saviour; but as Brethren, descended from the same ancestors, who speak the same language, adopt the same articles and ritual, and acknowledge the same orders.

We thank God, also, for his abundant mercy vouchsafed to them of late in the outpouring of His Holy Spirit; for the revival among them of sound and fervent piety; and for their zealous and devoted efforts in the cause of missions.

We earnestly pray that these great blessings may long be experienced by them; and that stimulated by their example, and seeking in the same spirit, we may ourselves in due season be visited by the same mercies—that our colleges may become seminaries at once of sound learning and religious education; and that our beloved Church may be yet, more than ever, a blessing and a praise in our land.

Retaining as we do the most affectionate remembrance of your late visit to our University, and accompanying you with our best wishes in all your labors for the Lord, we can not but request your prayers in return, that the Lord of the Harvest may bless the good seed which He permitted you to sow here; and that many laborers may be sent out from the midst of us into the wide harvest of the world.

Thus may our respective countries be one in blessings—in labors—and in love,—and animated, henceforth, with the only rivalry of holy zeal for the glory of our common Lord, may we provoke one another to love and to good works, and put forth our united energies to the spreading of the knowledge of the Redeemer's love.

Believe me, my dear friend, ever yours, very affectionately in Christian bonds,

                WILLIAM CARUS.

To the RIGHT REV. BP. McILVAINE.

We beg to express to Bishop McIlvaine our concurrence in the sentiments of the foregoing letter.

Signed,   C. SIMEON, M. A., *of King's College,*

       CHARLES PERRY, M. A., *Fellow and Assistant*

                Tutor of Trinity College,

And eighty-seven others, Members and Undergraduates of thirteen different Colleges.

The following is the answer of the Students of Kenyon College to the University of Oxford—that to Cambridge being to the same effect.

To Messrs. George Trevor, J. E. Giles, and Others, Bachelors and Undergraduates of the University of Oxford.

Gentlemen—The undersigned, Students in Theology, and Undergraduates of Kenyon College, have received through our President, the Rt. Rev. Bp. McIlvaine, the expression of your affectionate dispositions toward us, and the Institutions of which we are members.

Rightly have you judged that such a token of your sympathy would not be unacceptable. Standing as we do, almost on the western limit of civilization in North America, it would be strange indeed did we not receive with the most kindly feelings a salutation so fraternal, sent across the broad Atlantic, from the Bachelors and Undergraduates of your venerable University.

We bear in mind that while our Alma Mater is but of yesterday, yours is, in antiquity, second only to one other, and yields in no other particular to any; and that while you number your thousands of fellow-students, we can not even count our hundreds. But together with this thought, your communication suggests and cherishes in our hearts the hope that, in time to come, men will regard our present small beginnings, as we now look back to the state of things at Oxford, when your predecessors, in the days of Alfred, began their labors.

We are led also, by your salutation, to recognize and feel the importance of our position. As Oxford, once small and feeble, has long been a blessing to the ends of the earth, why may it not be believed, that Kenyon is called to the same high destiny; and through the smiles of God upon the encouragement and aid of our British friends, and upon our own vigorous exertions, will yet fulfil it. The world is before us all, as the wide and inviting field of benevolent exertion; and it is our desire, as being one with you in origin, language, literature, and religion—having "one Lord, one faith, one baptism"—to be one also in all the great efforts of Christian enterprise. And should Kenyon become, in the Providence of God, a source of blessing, in any measure, to this continent, it will be no small gratification to her sons, that multitudes from the very country which so generously helped to lay her foundations and erect her walls, will be partakers in the benefit, and thus enjoy some of the privileges of learning and religion, the loss of which is so keenly felt by the intelligent British emigrants. We are bound, also, to say, that to the exercise of such feelings we are incited, in addition to the considerations mentioned, by your affectionate sympathy, and that of many others, with our Rt. Rev. President, during his recent anxious mission to Great Britain. From his own lips, publicly and privately, we have heard of the many kind offices toward him on the part of our English brethren, and of their carnet desires for his success; and have felt it all as if it had been personal to ourselves.

Allow us then, gentlemen, to conclude this note with the expression of our best wishes for your individual happiness, and with the utterance of a fervent prayer, that amid the changes which are multiplying so rapidly throughout the world, a desecrating foot may never be allowed to enter your learned retreats; but that Oxford may ever stand unimpaired in her resources, and undiminished in her glory, the patroness of literature, and the champion of all Scriptural truth and order, uniting with her deep erudition the same spirit of brotherly kindness and charity which breathes in your communication to Kenyon College.

We are, Gentlemen, with sincere respect,

YOUR FRIENDS AND BRETHREN.

THE CRISIS OF 1842.

The sum contributed in England, $12,370, after defraying the Bishop's expenses, was to be sacredly applied to the building of Bexley Hall. It afforded, therefore, no relief from an oppressive debt. The collection in Ohio, by Dr. Sparrow, was only enough to discharge pressing claims, and keep down interest for a short time.

Still, had usual prosperity attended the Institution, its credit might have been sustained some time longer. But about the year 1840, several untoward events occurred. There was a gradual falling off of students from the South, and from the pecuniary depression of the times, and other causes, not enough presented themselves from the North and West to fill their places. Receipts from tuition were therefore very much diminished, while salaries and other expenses remained nearly the same as before.

Some revenue had been realized from the land, of which about 1,500 acres were under improvement; but there were so many drawbacks and losses, that in a series of years the actual amount was small.

In 1840 a change was made with a view of realizing a profit from grazing and raising cattle and sheep. But after expensive stock had been purchased, a dry season cut off the means of keeping it, and it was necessary to sell, at a great loss, to save life. There were those who blamed this experiment; but perhaps they would not have done so, if it had been attempted at a time when stock was rising, instead of falling, and when feed was plenty, instead of scarce. At such a time it might have cleared off the whole debt; but as it was, the profits went the wrong way.

Disastrous as this attempt was, it is perhaps well that it was tried, and equally well that it failed. As it is, the Trustees of Kenyon College, having tried in every way that appeared feasible, for twenty years, to make their farm sustain the Institution, and found it constantly sinking in debt, at length (some ten years since), came to the conclusion, that a religious corporation can not conduct a farm to advantage.

From the operation of the above causes, the year 1842 was the most gloomy one in the whole history of the Institution. The debt of Prime, Ward & King, then nearly $20,000, was pressing for liquidation. The land was mortgaged to secure it; and as financial affairs were then, the whole domain would scarcely more than have paid the debt.

It seemed a most inauspicious time to appeal to the public for aid, but it was determined to try; this being the only resource for saving the property of the Institution. In this emergency, our good Bishop put on the harness, and girded himself for the work of begging. An appeal, called "*An Earnest Word*," was issued, the style and purport of which, as well as the purpose for which aid was asked, may be learned from the following extract: "The 4,000 acres of land making the endowment, in the center of which the buildings stand, the rents of which are depended on for support, * * are considered worth in common times from 80 to 100,000 dollars. The buildings owned by the Institution, thereupon, are estimated as worth at least 75,000 dollars. The latter, of course, are of no use for the payment of debt. They are worth nothing but for a college. We must keep them or perish. The landed endowment is all that could be used for the payment of debt. Suppose it sold? It must *all* be sold to raise money enough in these times to meet the case; or, at the very best, so large a part (and that the most valuable) must be sold, as entirely to ruin the endowment."—*An Earnest Word*, p. 4.

The Rev. Mr. Lounsbury was employed as an agent to present the cause in Ohio, and he and the Rev. Mr. Clark to assist Bishop McIlvaine at the East.

The application to raise money to save the endowment of the Theological Seminary of Ohio and Kenyon College succeeded well, as the following subscription lists will show. This successful effort has rightly conferred on Bishop McIlvaine the title of Second Founder of the Institution—a work really more trying than had ever yet been undertaken for Kenyon College.

The following is copied and arranged from the original subscription-book belonging to Bishop McIlvaine:

NEW YORK.

Adee, G. T	$100
Agnew, J.	6
Alsop, J. W	50
Anstice, Henry	20
Anthon, Rev. Dr	50
Arcularius, A	20
Ascension Church, collection	281
Ascension, two ladies of	58
Ascension, friends of, by the Rector	30
Aspinwall, James S	50
Aspinwall, W. H	200
Babcock, N	10
Babcock, Mrs	10
Baff, Mrs	2
Banyer, Mrs	250
Benjamin, John	10
Bogart, H. K	5
Bogg, Mrs. Sarah	100
Bradish, Mrs	26
Bridge, L. K	50
Bridgeman, Mr	1
Brown, Stewart	200
Burret, T	5
Butler, A	25
Cash	10
"	6
"	5
"	5
" through Dr. Milnor	5
" by Mr. Cornell	7
Carm, Isaac	200
Clark, Gerardus	100
Clerk, a (St. Mark's)	10
Chauncey, H	100
Cloud, J	5
Cook, Levi	25
Davies, H. E.	15
De Forest, Mr	5
De Peyster, F	100
Dominick, James W	100
Dominick, collected by	120
Douglas, George	250

Dubois, C	$100
Dubois, C., jr	50
Earle, J. E.	10
Edmunds, F. W	20
Ely, Charles	50
Faile, F. H.	100
Fish, Hamilton	50
Fish, Mrs. Col	50
Friend, through S. Browne	200
"	20
"	15
Furness, M. P	200
Garner, T	100
Gordon, O. H	50
Gould, E. S	10
Grosvenor, Jasper	100
H	4 40
Hadden, David	100
Haggarty, D	25
Haggarty, John & Son	100
Haight, E	5
Hale, Josiah	20
Hastings, George	50
Herrick, J. B	50
Hewlet, Joseph	20
Holbrook, E	10
Holmes, S. H	20
Hopkins, R. H	20
Hubbell, H. W	10
Hyslop, R	10
Jay, Hon. Wm., Esq	50
Jay, John	5
Jay, Miss	300
Jay, Miss S	1
Jones, D. T. & Co	100
Kane, Delancy	5
Kermott, R	50
King, S. G.	100
Kluts, George	5
Lady, a	50
Lady, a	40
Leroy, Jacob	100
Leroy, Jacob R	100
Livingston, Schuyler	25

Little, Mr., St. Stephen's, 2d gift	$5	
Loder, B.	100	
Lothrop, W. K.	10	
Lorillard, Miss	500	
Lorillard, P. Jr.	500	
Lossing, J. B.	5	
Loudon, E.		50
Loyd, J. J.	28	
Mason, Rev. C.	10	
McVicker, Dr.	12	
Maitland, W. C.	25	
Merritt, Miss	14	
Milligan, W.	25	
Milnor, Rev. Dr.	220	
Minturn, R. B.	200	
Mosier, J	50	
Morehouse, Mrs	2	
Morrill, T.	10	
Myers, Mrs., Fourteenth St.	5	
Nelson, William	10	
Noble, Mrs	5	
Ogden, J. D. P.	50	
Olmsted, F. W.	50	
Packwood, N.	10	
Passom, W.	5	
Pattison, Godfrey	25	
Pennel, Dr.	5	
Phalan, James	20	
Porter, E.	5	
Rhea, Mrs. Richard	100	
Rogers, S. J.	10	
Russel, Israel	5	
Sabine, Mrs.	10	
Sanderson, E. F.	50	
Sands, J., Esq., & Co.	170	
Sanford, L.	5	
Schuchard, F.	25	
Seymore, McNeil	10	
Sheafe, J. P. & S. F.	200	
Sheldon, Henry	50	
Simmons, W. P.	50	
Skeel, Mrs. Rufus R.	25	
Spencer, Capt. W. A.	100	
Spicer, Mrs	10	
Stagg, J. P.	100	
Stewart, A. T.	50	
Stamford & Co., through	237	43
St. George's, collection	160	16
St. George's, member of.	5	
St. Mark's, collection	200	
St. Stephen's, member of, (by Dr. A.)	2	
St. Stephen's, member of.	3	
Storm, G.	10	
Stout, A. G.	10	
Stuyvesant, P. G.	200	
Suydam, Mrs.	5	
Taylor, Jeremiah H.	10	
Thome, G. F.	10	
Tiffany, S. T.	10	
Trowbridge, F. W.	10	

Tufnel, Capt. and Mrs.	$4	
Turner, Miss	10	
Waddell, Charles	10	
Wagstaff, Dr.	25	
Waldron, William,	5	
Ward, A. P.	50	
Watts, Mr. John	100	
Watts, Mrs. Ann	100	
West, Edward D.	20	
Wetmore, Prosper M.	20	
Wetmore, W. S.	200	
Whitlock, Wm.	50	
Willis, Edward	20	
Winthrop, R.	100	
Woolley, P. L., per	115	
Wolfe, Christopher	50	
Wolfe, J. D.	200	
Wood, R. W.	10	

BROOKLYN.

Abraham, James	5	
Abraham, Mrs. Jane	5	
Acosta, John	50	
Adams, J. C.	5	
Arnold, D. N.	25	
Austin, David	50	
B. D. D.	5	
Bill, Cyrus	25	
Brown, Mrs. Matilda	25	
Burton, O. D.	10	
Calvary Church, collection	50	80
Christ Church, ladies of	31	
" " collection	50	56
Cash, four items	65	85
Cooper, William B	50	
Chew, T. J.	30	
Cowly, J. A.	10	
Cornell, Whitehead J., Esq.	100	
Cornell, P. C.	100	
Dickinson, Mr.	1	
Doughty, John S.	20	
Dubois, Dr.	120	
Dunham, E. W.	100	
Embury, A. B.	10	
Emmanuel Church	100	
Goddard, Rev. K., by	20	
Gibson, Alexander	10	
Harper, A. M.	10	
J. A.	10	
Jarvis, George A	5	
Ketchum, Captain	10	
Luquier, Nicholas	50	
Marvin, C. R.	10	
Matthew, A. D.	10	
McClellan, C. R.	10	
Messenger, Thomas	25	
Middleton, T. D.	10	
Miller, W. S.	20	
Morsell, James S.	20	
Neely, James M	5	
Peet, F. T.	100	
Perkins, J. W.	100	

Pettit, Joseph	$50	
Pettit, Robert	20	
Pierrpont, Miss Anne	100	
Pierrpont, Miss F.	100	
Pierrpont, Mary M.	50	
Pierrpont, H.	100	
Robinson, James	5	
Soley, E.	5	
Sands, J. & Co.	170	
Sands, Mr. J.	2	50
Skidmore, S. T.	5	
Smith, Miss Phebe	5	
Stanton, C.	30	
St. Ann's, member of	41	
" collection	79	11
" cash	1	
St. Felix, Charles A.	10	
St. Mary's Church, per rector,	10	
Stebbins, D. M.	20	
Stone, Rev. Dr., per	112	
Taylor, C. J.	30	
Trenchard, Mrs.	2	50
Ten Eyck, Mrs.	5	
Tucker, Richard S.	50	
Tucker, Thatcher	5	
Upjohn, Richard	50	
Van Pelt, Mrs.	5	
Widow's Mite	2	50
Wood, Miss	5	
Webster, Hosea	100	
Wilmerding, W. E.	.50	
Wood, Ransom E.	50	
Worthington, Rossiter	5	

BOSTON.

A. B. C.	10	
Andrews, H.	20	
Andrews, James	5	
Appleton, Robert	10	
Appleton, William	500	
Armory, James A.	25	
Armory, William	25	
Aspinwall, A.	20	
Blake, Ed.	5	
Blanchard. James	5	
Bradford, William B.	5	
Brimmer, Martin	50	
Brimmer, Miss Eliza	50	
Brown, C.	10	
Bush, Mr., per	5	
Cash, per W. B. Reynolds	5	50
" two gifts	15	
Caznove. Mrs. S. E.,	5	
Chamberlain, D.	20	
Clark, B. C.	10	
Codman, C. R.	100	
Codman, F.	25	
Codman. Henry	100	
Coffin, Miss	20	
Daniel, Otis	50	
Dehon, William.	5	
Eastburn, Bishop	100	

Farley, Robert	$50	
Friends, six	55	
Green. J. Copley, and family,	400	
Greenleaf, Prof.	10	
Hale, Dr.	5	
Holbrook, J. G.	50	
Howard, B.	50	
Hubbard, Mrs. J.	20	
Hunt, Miss Philomela	2	
Jarvis, Dr.	25	
Jeffries, Dr	25	
Lady, by Dr. Vinton	1	50
Lady	12	
Lawrence, Amos, sen	25	
Lawrence, Amos	100	
Loyd, Mrs.	20	
Mason, Jeremiah	20	
Oden, George	10	
Otis, W. P.	20	
Parker, Charles W.	10	
Parker, Charles H.	5	
Patton, James	10	
Peters, Ed. D.	50	
Rand, Ed. L.	20	
Reed, B. T.	25	
Richardson, Benj. P	25	
Sargent, L. M.	20	
Shattuck, Dr., jr	50	
Shelton, P. S.	10	
St. Paul's Church	110	81
Thaxter, Adam W.	20	
Tracey. Nathaniel	10	
Thorndike, Mrs.	25	
Trimmins. Henry	50	
Warner, J. S.	100	
Watts, Francis O.	20	
Watts, Mrs.	2	
Widow's Mite	1	50

PHILADELPHIA.

Biddle. Mrs.	5	
Cash, by Miss McIlvaine	1	
Childs, Col.	5	
Clericus	100	
Cresson, Mrs. Marg.	5	
Day, S., Esq., for several, of St. Andrew's	54	60
Evangelist, Church of, by Rev. Mr. Quinan	10	
Epiphany, per Dr. Tyng	50	
" A. Barrington,	2	50
" Mrs. Cotton....	10	
" Miss Elvin	20	
" Mrs. Hughes,...	5	
" Dr. King	10	
" J. Hockley.	5	
" M. P. F.	50	
" Mite	5	
" Dr. Morris	10	
" C. R. Thompson	25	
.. one sovereign..	4	80
" collection	700	

Grace Church, collection.......$845 50
Godey, Mrs., by N. McIlvaine.   5
Hull, Rev. A., per.............   7 92
Learning, friend of..............   20
Lady, St. Peter's...................   5
Lady   15
Ladies, two, per N. McIlvaine.   25
McKnight, Miss.................   5
Recorder, through.......... .... 1105 32
Rush, Mrs   10
St. Andrew's, by C. Stevenson   30
    "   . Female Com'c't.   20
    "   Members of......   65 10
St. Luke's, collection.............   270
    "   Member of Cong...   117
St. Paul's.........   405
St. Philip's........................   805
Stott, Mrs.. Eliza...... .....:..   200
Williams, Henry S.............   20

PROVIDENCE.

Adams, Seth, jr 50
Allen, Miss Candace...........   30
Allen, P...........................   25
Allen, C. & Co.....................   20
Barstow, John.....................   20
Burgess, Thomas..................   30
Chapin, Armory...................   20
Clarke, Mrs. H. M.............   5
Dabney, C. H.....................   20
Foster, Mrs. M. M.............   5
Foster, Freeman........   5
Friend..............................   25
Goddard, Wm. G...............   100
Grinnell, W. T......... .... -.... 20
Gurney, Austin.....................   10
Howard, E. W......................   25
Hoskins, James H.............   2
Ives, Mrs. Hope......   30
Ives, Robert H......................   100
Ives, Harriet B...............   25
Kelley, W.............................   10
Manton, A   12
Moore, John Carter......   10
Potter, Charles....................   20
St. John's, ladies of..............   100
    "   collection.............   91 15
Thompson, Lydia...................   10

Newport, cash per Lounsbury. 125
Lady, per. W. K. Newman...   50
Zion Church, member of......   5

BALTIMORE.

A Lady............ 10
Armstrong, James.....   6
Armstrong, James Dunn.......   10
Brown, George.....................   25
Bash, Mr., per J. Loney.........   10
Boyle, Mrs...... 10
Bradshaw, Mr., Chr. Ch.......   1
Cash...... 14

Chapin, Rev. A. R., per......... $ 15
Carrol, James......   10
Christ Church...................   112 07
Chr. Ch., per Rev. Mr. Bean.   70
Currie, William................ ...   100
Hooper, J.........................   5
Herring, Henry   1
Johns, John.......................   100
Lady, per R. S. Coxe............   5
Loney, J..........................   20
Lippit, Rev., per............ ....   76 07
Mantz, Louisa...:.................   2
Mankin, Israel, St. Peter's......   20
Mankin, John,   "   5
Metcalf, John   "   10
Miner, Mrs.........................   5
Merrit, Christ Church..........   50
Mite, E............................   5
M. L., Miss.........................   1
Pollock, Wm......:.....   5
Presbyterian.......................   5
Ridgely, Mrs. John...........   15
Ridgely, Mrs. D..................   5
Scott, John   5
Scott, Mrs. E.....................   5
Scott, Mrs. Elizabeth G........ ...   5
Smith, Edward......................   1
St. Peter's 265 25
St. Peter's, Ladies' Soc........   100
Spicer, Thos,. H., St. Peter's...   25
Taylor, Robert R..................   20
Tilghman, Mr. and Miss, and
    Miss Owen....................   10
Thorn, Mr   5
Thomas, Mrs. S. K......:.....   5
Thompson, Capt., per............   298 15
    "   "   "   38
Widow's mite....................   2 50
Woodward, Wm.......   10

WASHINGTON.

Brook, W. & M....... ....,..   10
Christ Church, member of...   20
Coxe, Mrs. Richard..............:   50
Coxe, R. S., Esq., per.........   20
Dayton, H. V..   10
D. C., per. Lounsbury   159
Dunbar, Mrs.....   2
Individuals ....,...........   20
Law, Mrs..........................   5
Lady, a...........................   5
Leur, Mrs.......................   10
Reed, Miss Mary.................   10
Scott, General....................   10
Smith, John A..........… ……   10
St. John's, per Rev. Mr. Hawley 21
Trinity Church, per. Mr. String-
    fellow.....................   42 50

FREDERICK.

Bircley, Maria   10
Cash....... ....,..   5

Gordon, F.	$ 10		Potts, R.	$ 10
Gray, John	10		Potts, Mrs. R.	10
Howard, Mrs.	25		Potts, Geo. M	10
Harney, John		50	Richardson, D.	5
Hamilton & Freeman	5		Ross, Wm.	5
Johnson, Dr. T. W	5		Ross, W. J	5
Lady, All Saints'	20		Stokes, R. G	5
McPherson, Miss	5		Tyler, Dr. William	10
Narni, Basil	10		Tyler, Dr. W	10
Phillips, Rev. R. H. R.	10			

MISCELLANEOUS.

NEW YORK.

Anonymous, Syracuse, per Rev. Dr. Gregory	$ 2	
Barclay, Henry, Newtown	10	
Childs, Col., U. S. A	5	
Clarkson, Rev. Mr., for the Church at Fishkill Landing.	50	
C. A. H. Miss, Syracuse, per Dr. Gregory	30	
C. L., Mr., per do	5	
Collection in St. Luke's Church Rochester	100	
Friend, Geneva	40	
Friend, Military Academy	3	
Granger, Gen. A. S., Syracuse, per Dr. Gregory	30	
Holly, W. W., Esq., Geneva	30	
Jaquer, Jehiel, Flushing	25	
M. M. Z., Fort Hamilton	25	
Peck, Elijah, Flushing	25	
Peck, Rev. Isaac, "	100	
St. Ann's Church, Fishkill Landing	50	
St. James' Church, monthly offering	15	
St. John's Church, Mt. Morris	30	
Smith, Capt. Samuel	5	
Tibbits, Mr. George, Troy	50	
Tibbits, Mrs. Geo., "	5	
Tibbits, Mrs., "	50	
Trinity Church, Geneva, friend of	70	
Trin. Church, Geneva, family of, per Rev. P. Irving	30	
Trin. Church, Geneva, members of	55	
Valk, J. R., Flushing	5	

MARYLAND AND D. C.

Chapman, Mrs. E. P., Port Tobacco	5	
Christ Church, Ladies of, Alexandria	7	
Christ Church, Georgetown, Missionary Society	3	50
Christ Church, Georgetown	44	
Collected by Miss Hayes, M't-		

gomery County Male S. S., Christ Church	$ 25	
Dana, Rev. Mr., Alexandria	20	
Friends, two, Prince George's County	15	
Goldsborough, Rev. Mr	5	
McGuire, Rev. Dr	5	
Presbyterian, Annapolis	10	
Robins, Rev. Mr	110	

MASSACHUSETTS.

St. James', Roxbury	60	
St. James', Marblehead, a few parishioners of	29	
St. Stephen's, Pittsfield	1	
Country clergyman	10	
Draft on Merchants' Bank Salem	170	

PENNSYLVANIA.

James L. Bowman, Brownville	100	
Jacob Bowman, "	100	
Mr. Bowman, "	2	
George Hogg	20	
St. Mark's S. S., Lewiston	3	14

NEW JERSEY.

Cash, Newark	13	
Samuel Meeker	10	
J. P. Pennington	10	
Charles Olden, Princeton	15	
John Potter, "	25	
James Potter, "	25	
Mary and Louisa Rutherford, "	200	
L. P. Smith, "	5	
Mrs. White, "	6	

CONNECTICUT.

Mr. Clark, Danbury	$. 1	
Christ Church, Hartford	187	
Christ Church, Watertown	1	
Church Offering, New Haven.	3	
St. James' Church, Derby	30	
St. John's, Hartford, three members.	11	
Trin. Church, Bromford	2	
Trin. Church, New Haven	69	68

VIRGINIA.

Barton, Dr. W., Winchester...	$ 10	
Bullock, Mrs., Richmond......	2	
Burwell, Philip........	5	
Clark county, per Rev. A. Clark.............	50	
Clarke, Mrs. H. M.............	5	
Church collection, Winchester.	48	69
Collected by Rev. Mr. Woodbridge	6	
Dougham, Rev. Mr., per.........	148	25
Episcopal High School, per Rev. Mr. Pendleton.............	50	
Foster, Mr. M. M......	5	
Gentleman.............	100	
Grammar. Rev. John...............	7	50
Hooe, Dr. Abraham, King George county, proceeds of land............ ... .1475		17
Johns, Bishop, per, Richmond.	20	
Jackson, Rev. Wm	5	
Lee, Mrs. E. M. P., by Rev. John Grammar,	3	
Leigh, Mrs. Rebecca, "	2	50
Love, Mrs. M. A., "	2	
Meade, Bishop......	100	
Meade, R. K., Milwood......	5	
Meade, Philip N., "	5	
Meade, Mrs., "	1	
Nelson, Miss E. H., "	4	
Nelson, Dr. Wm., "	5	
Robertson, Mr......	5	
Robinson, Mr......	5	
Robins, Rev. John.............	40	
Southern Churchman, per......	25	
Stuart, Mrs. Martha C., King George county, proceeds of land	785	58
Williams, Philip, Winchester..	10	
Williams, Miss Mary......... ......$	1	

SOUTH CAROLINA.

Bishop Gadsden......	5	
Barnwell, Rev. Mr., Charleston.	15	
Beaufort, St. Helen's Church...	280	
St. Michael's, Charleston......	7	
Sundry persons, per Rev. Mr. Barnwell, Charleston.........	115	50
Weston, Francis M., Georgetown............	100	
Weston, F. B., per	15	

MICHIGAN.

Baldwin, H. P., Detroit.........	5	
Fitch, Rev. C. W......	5	
Trowbridge, Mrs. E............ ...	10	
Trowbridge, Miss E.	5	
Trowbridge, C. C............... ...	10	

OTHER STATES.

Mrs. Monroe, Arlington, Vt...	5	
Rev. C. E. Leverett, Edisto Island, N. C............	100	
Collected in the south by Mr. Lounsbury.	286	66
St. Paul's Church, New Orleans, La............	30	
St. John's, Savannah, Ga......	1	
H. Delano, Henderson, Ky.....	20	
Rev. Geo. Fox, Durham, Eng.	100	
Collected by Rev. E. Lounsbury, without names.	558	99
" " " ".	75	
Donation of Rev. E. Lounsbury.	25	
J. W. Allen, Cleveland, O......	10	
From different persons to pay interest.........	1246	

This last item, together with the donations of Dr. Hooe and his sister, Mrs. Stuart, of Va., amounting in all to $3,456 75, were not included in Bishop McIlvaine's account in 1843, because, though these sums belong to the results of the same effort, the money was not received by him, and had not been realized at the time.

The net result of this effort, including $130 from Ohio, was the sum of $29,516 60.

After the final report of Bishop McIlvaine, of the results of this collection, the following resolutions were passed by the Board of Trustees, being appended to a report of a committee, which concludes thus:

" The widow's mite and the rich man's gift have each been cheerfully thrown into the treasury, and the donors have thus, we trust, lent to the Lord that which he will repay them. The Bishop's account of his stewardship is full and satisfactory. He went forth literally without money and without scrip, but his trust was in the Lord, from whom cometh every good and perfect gift. The result has been already stated, and it only remains for the committee to submit the following resolutions :

"1. *Resolved,* That the Board does, and will ever cherish, a most grateful recollection af the generous kindness of our eastern brethren and friends, who, in our hour of need, have so largely helped the great interests of Christian education in this Diocese ; and the Secretary is hereby directed to preserve and file, among the archives of the Theological Seminary at Gambier, the statement book and vouchers now communicated by the Bishop, exhibiting the sources from whence the generous aid was received, and the uses made of it.

"2. *Resolved further,* That our Rt .Rev. Bishop McIlvaine has most ably and faithfully discharged the laborious and highly-important trust thus devolved upon him. And this Board have heard with inexpressible pleasure, from other reliable sources at the East, that this arduous duty was performed, not only with signal ability, but with a Christian spirit and zeal which, under. his Master's direction, made many new friends for the vast interests under his charge.

"3. *Resolved further,* That this Board hereby assure the Bishop that they entertain a most grateful sense of the valuable and important services which he has rendered, not only to the Theological Seminary, and to the College, but to the great interests of the Church in this. Diocese. And while the Bishop declines all pecuniary remuneration, nothing having been retained therefor beyond his mere personal expenses, the Trustees do insist, and hereby most respectfully beg him to retain and keep, for his own use, the small balance, ($207 16,) which, as before stated, he has reported as unexpended and subject to order, and for that purpose the Secretary is hereby directed to make out and deliver to the Bishop, in the name and behalf of this Board, the proper receipt and voucher. All which is respectfully submitted.'

WM. KEY BOND, Chairman.

THE APPLICATION IN OHIO RESULTED IN THE FOLLOWING COLLECTIONS IN 1843.

CINCINNATI.

Adams, W. L.	$ 20
Andrews, William	20
Aydelotte, Rev. B. P.	5
Bond, Wm. Key	100
Bishop, S.	20
Bowler, R. B.	100
Boylon, B.	5
Brooke, Rev. J. T.	100
Buchanan, R.	25
Burrows, J. D.	25
Cash, live items, $5 each	25
Cash, three items, $3 each	9
Cash, two items, $2 each	4
Cady, D. K.	25
Chase, Salmon P.	5
Clark, Henry	25
Christ Church, a lady of	50
Christ Church, Ben. Soc.	50
Cragg, R.	2
Cromwell, N.	10
Davidson, Tyler	100
Dudley, Clara	20
Este, D. K.	240
Fore, P. G.	30
Garrett, A.	10
Gorman, J.	50
Gregory, Walter	50
Gwynne, David	120
Haynes, E. S.	100
Holbrook, Wm. R.	25
Hall, James	10
Hall, Jas. C.	25
Hewson, B. W.	10
Hodges, R.	100
Irwin, A.	100
Irwin, J. T.	10
Jones, John D.	120
Jones, Mr. Geo. W.	25
Jones, Talbott	25
Keith, James, jr	10
Kenner, Geo. R.	100
Kilgore, John	120
King, Rufus	10
Kinneer, John	10
L'Hommedieu, Samuel	10
Lockwood, E. S.	10
Miller, W.	20
Miner, John L.	25
Neave, C.	50
Nixon, W.	1
Norris, N.	20
Oliver, Will	25
Pendleton, N. G.	200
Pomeroy, S. W.	120
Pullen, Joseph	5
Richards, Wolcott	20
Richards, Susan	5

Rockey, H.	20
Rowe, Stanhope S.	$ 20
Shulk, Charles	20
Smith, J. Howard, U. S. N.	10
Smith, W. B.	10
Shoenberger, G. K.	240
Storer, B.	100
Strader, D. O.	10
Strader, Jacob	240
Taylor, Griffin	240
" "	100
Van Doren, J. L.	50
Van Mater, Daniel	5
Walker, J. H.	2
Wharton, R. J.	10
Wright, C. L.	3
Woodrow, D. T.	10
Worthington, E.	20
Yardly, K.	50

TROY, MIAMI CO.

Barrett, Thomas S.	4
Bayless, S. D.	5
Cash	3
Clemens, Asa	10
Mayo, H. S.	10
McClung, J. T.	1

PIQUA.

Adams, Demas, jr.	25
Alexander, A. C.	25
Brownell, R. L.	120
Clewell, Mrs.	5
Conrad, Daniel P.	15
Dorsey, J. Volney	20
Ferrall, J. O.	20
Horton, D.	10
Killin, Rev. R. S.	15
Kirk, William R.	10
Knowles, William	10
Johnston, John	100
Johnston, Mrs. Mary	5
Johnston, G. C.	50
McCorkle, Mrs.	10
Mitchell, M. G.	20
Morrow, John	10
Scott, William	30
Starrett, James	25
Vaile, John	10

SPRINGFIELD.

Bean, J. A.	2
Coles, W.	5
Cunning, E. H.	90
Ludlow, John	5
Mitter, Mrs.	1
Moore, Benjamin	3
Presbury, Rev. Willard	5
Smallwood, Walter A.	5

Sykes, James.................... $ 3	Little, William*................$120
Warwood, Thomas J..... 2	Sharpe, Mr...... 5

PORTSMOUTH.

JOHNSTOWN.

Buchanan, H*................... 120	B. W. Pratt................. 20
Burr, Rev. E................. 40	

CHILLICOTHE.

Cay, C. M........ : 10	
Cash...... 5	Adams, Samuel........... 10
Child, A. L... 6	Bethell, Robert...... 10
Clark, S.... 1	Britton, Rev. J. B..... 25
Conway, B. F................ 3	Caldwell, J. D.................. 5
Damarin, C. A. M.......... 5	Cash...... 1
Davis, James W.......... 5	Coones, Mrs. E................ 100
Fumstone. J. G.............. 10	Creed, George................. 5
Gillett, John.......... 2	Davis, E. H...., ... 5
Hall, Mr....... 40	Doddridge, B. Z. B........... 5
Hamilton, Edward............ 10	Douglas, Luke....... 20
Henking, C................. 3	Douglas, Mrs. W. U......... ... 5
Kelsoe, M.......... 5	Fairbanks, B.... 5
Kinney, A.......... 50	Foulke, L. W................. 10
Kinney, E.......... 25	Joline, C. A.............. 5
Kinney, P................. 50	Kendrick, E. P.*...... 60
Kinney, P. C................ 5	Kirchaval, J. A................ 10 -
Kinney, W.*................. 120	Madeira, John....... 50
Little Girl............. 50	McGinnis, Ann Eliza...... 5
Lodwick, James.......... 50	McGinnis, Hannah M......... 5
Masting, F. M............... 2	McGinnis, Charles J........... 5
Masting, T. M............... 5	Marfield, John*............... 60
Pressel, D. W............... 1	Martin, C..................... 3
Ross, M. B............ 5	Parker, Joseph N........... 5
Scott, D.. 5	Reeves, C. T.*............... 60
Shewell. E.......... 1	Scott, Charles L........... 5
Smith, L. P. M.............. 2	Scott, G............. 20
Spencer, Thomas............... 5	Scott, Mrs..................... 5
Tomlinson, L. E................ 1	Strong, Wm. Y...... 5
Westwood, Daniel...... 1	Thatcher, N. W................ 10
	Watts, John........, ... 10

GRANVILLE.

	Wood, John...... 200
Bronson, Rev. S. A.............. 1	Woodbridge, J................ 150
Head, Miss Catherine.......... 1	
Johnson, Miss Fidelia.......... 2	**MT. VERNON.**
Pratt, Miss Julia A............. 2	
Prichard, A. P................. 5	Alling, E................ 10
Prichard, Miss Caroline... 1	Brown, A. H................ 20
Richards, W. S............. 1	Buckingham, C. P.*........... 120
Sanford, Rev. A......... 50	Burr, J. N................. 20
	Clark, Russel......... .... 5 50

NEWARK.

	Curtis, H. B.*.................. 120
Dickinson, L. A. H...... 20	Curtis, H. & Son.............. 15
Franklin, Mr................. 2	Delano, C.*................. 120
Penney, G. W............... 10	Durbin, Thomas......... 5
Richards, William.............. 10	Evans, Job................... 10
Sprague, H. S...... 30	Fairchild, D. S. & Co........... 15
Taylor, John...... 10	Huntsberry, James... 20
Warner, Luke K............... 5	Irvine, J. C................. 20
	Miller, Hon. Elie...... .... 28 14
	Miller, J. W................ 10

DELAWARE.

	Morrison, James......... 40
Andrews, H. G................ 10	Raymond, H. A............... 10
Chamberlin, C. C. 10	Stamp, M. W.*................ 120
Dyke, Daniel.................. 1	Stockton, John C....... 48
Howard, C. 40	Voorhies, S. T................ 10

GAMBIER.

Fobes, A. K.	$5
Gibbs, Charles	25
Gwin, E. M.	5
McIlvaine, Rt. Rev. C. P.	100
Mulford, Annanius	5
Myers, G. W.	5
Sawer, J. S.	5
Scott, A. G.	10
Trimble, John (Perry)	15
White, M.	10
Wing, Rev. M. T. C.	50

COLUMBUS.

Buttles, A.	50
Whiting, I. N.	100

HURON.

Caldwell, Joseph	10
Christ Church, collection	10
Wickham, John W.	30

SANDUSKY.

Barber, A. H.	6
Barker, Z. W.	10
Bangle, A.	1
Bush, Davis	10
Caswell, W. H.	2
Chapman, W. P.	3
Grace Church, collection	5
Haines, E. H.	5
Harper, Rice	15
Higgins, Burr*	120
Hollister, J. W.	10
Schook, James	12
Sloane, J. N.	10
Taylor, James	1

NORWALK.

Boalt, C. L.	25
Boalt, Eben	15
Bowes, John R.	20
Cash	5
Cash	1
Cheesebrough	5
Lewis, Samuel B.	10
Patrick, Shepherd	30
Pomeroy, Samuel, jr.	5

GRAFTON.

Fisher, Charles	3
Sibley, George	3
Turner, Wm.	3

COLUMBIA.

Adams, Mr.	1	
Nicholas, Simeon	2	
Squiers, Mr.	1	25

LIVERPOOL.

Christ Church	20
Woodward, H. S.	10

MEDINA.

Badger, Austin	$4	
Bronson, Hiram	15	
Bronson, Isaac	5	
Canfield, W. H.	25	
Clark, John L.	5	
Hiccox, Wm.	5	
Horton, Seth.	4	
Mrager, Russel	5	
Root, Mr.		50
Simmons, D. B., and others	10	
Sargent, S. N.	10	
Warren, E. H.	1	
Welton, E.	1	
Welton, E. E.	5	
Welton, S. B.	5	
Willard, G. T.	2	50

STRONGSVILLE.

Northrop, B.	30

DOVER.

Adams, L. L.	2	
Hall, Charles	5	
Lilley, Luther	1	
Smith, Clark	2	50

OHIO CITY.

Bevertin, John	1
Degman, Mr.	1
Randla, Mrs.	3
Russell, Mrs.	1

ELYRIA.

Andrews, Lucy	3
Andrews, Mary J.	2
Cowles, Orrin	30
Leonard, E. H.	10
Starr, Raymond	6
Tiffany, J.	6

LYME.

McCurdy, Richard L.	2
Woodward, Rachel	1

WOOSTER.

Graham, Wm.	6
Schmucker, J. W.	6

MANSFIELD.

Bowman, S.	10
Johns, B.	25

NEW HAVEN.

Crowell, T. W.	10
McEwen, T. C.	5

MONROE FALLS.

Cartwright, Ellen M.	5
Cartwright, John W.	3
Comstock, Calvin	5
Fox, Mr.	1

Gaylord, Isaac T.............. .... $5
Rattle, S.......... 5
Weld, Ellen W.......... 2
Willis, Edward P.......... 2

Wolcott, Frederick.......... .... $10

NEWTON FALLS.

Dr. H. N. Dubois *.......... 120

MISCELLANEOUS.

St. Timothy's Church, Massillon *.......... ....$120
Martin Andrews, Steubenville *.......... 120
Donation,   "   1
Miss Mary Hammond, "   25
Bazaleel Wells.......... 10
Trinity Parish, Jefferson.......... 10
Rev. John Bryan, Windsor.......... 5
Donations without names, Cleveland.......... .... 267 50
S. C. Beaver, Coshocton 5
Mrs. Hazlett, Zanesville.......... 3
Mr. Lake, Oxford.......... 1
George Hogg, Brownsville, Pa. *.... ...., ... 120

Of the above subscription, the sums marked * were subscriptions for which scrip was issued, entitling the bearer to an equivalent in tuition, or, after five years, to demand the money. Hence $3,150 of the above was a loan, and has since been accounted for, leaving the Ohio donation of 1843, $5,785.39, which, added to the sum obtained at the East, makes the whole result of the effort of 1843, $35,302; and deducting $302 for expense of collecting $8,911.39 in Ohio, leaves it $35,000. So much was obtained from a benevolent public to save the endowment of these Institutions.

SCHOLARSHIP FUND, OBTAINED IN 1850, BY REV. J. MUEN-SCHER, D. D.

In the year 1850, a subscription was taken up in Ohio, amounting to $11,924, called a "*Subscription to Scholarship Fund.*" It was intended by this effort to found a professorship by the sale of scholarships. The condition was that the subscriber on paying $200 should receive a certificate entitling the holder to tuition in any department of the Institution. Upon this subscription was collected the sum of $5,600, and certificates therefor have been issued. This is, in effect, a loan, on which interest is payable in tuition.

A few subscribers, having paid in part, compromised by surrendering their claim to scholarships, and thus obtained a release

5

from payment of the balance. What was paid, therefore, should be considered as donations. These sums are as follows:

Bishop McIlvaine	$133 33
H. Matthews	30 00
S. M. Sanford	100 00
James Hall	40 00
E. T. Stirling	200 00
	$503 33

LIBRARY AND APPARATUS.

The Catalogue of the Theological Seminary and College, for 1860, makes the following statement respecting Libraries:

The Libraries to which the students have access are as follows, viz :

1. The Library of the Seminary and College, containing 6,500 volumes.
2. That of the Philomathesian Society, containing 3,527 volumes.
3. That of the Nu Pi Kappa Society, containing 3,357 volumes.

The Libraries of the Societies have been accumulated and mainly given by the students themselves. To name the donors would require a catalogue of a greater part of all the students that have ever been connected with the Institution.

Of the donors to the Library of the Seminary it will be practicable here to name only a few.

Through Bishops Chase and McIlvaine, extensive and valuable collections of books were received from England.

P. G. Stuveysant, of New York, besides liberal subscriptions otherwise, gave $1,000 in money to increase the library.

Charles D. Betts, of New York, left, for charitable purposes, in the hands of Dr. Anthon, the sum of $1,000. This sum was given by him, the interest of which is to be applied, under the direction of the Faculty, to the purchase of Theological books.

Rollin Sandford, Esq., and Messrs. Carter & Brothers, of N. Y., have more recently presented some eighty volumes each, of valuable books.

It will not be practicable here to name all the valuable gifts that have been made to aid the scientific departments of the College.

In addition to the gifts received from England, already mentioned, C. L. Boalt, Esq., of Norwalk, in 1849, gave $100, and Rev. C. C. Pinckney, of South Carolina, gave $200 to fit up a laboratory. These gifts were very opportune, and received with special thankfulness, because they came when few were disposed to give.

Since then, a choice portable cabinet of utensils for testing minerals has been received from Rev. S. A. Bronson, and a telescope and transit instrument from Rev. Peter Neff, jr. These instruments presented to the Observatory were, an Achromatic Telescope, seven and a half inches diameter, eight and a half feet focal length, mounted equatorially, furnished with clock movement and various eye-pieces. It is now mounted under the revolving dome, in the tower of "Ascension Hall." Also, a Transit instrument, made by E. & G. W. Blunt, of New York. The Telescope (two inches aperture, and about two feet focal length) is a very accurate and finely-made instrument.

As the above gifts are specific, and were appropriated by the donors, and are now in a shape in which their value can not be measured by money, they will not hereafter be embraced in allusion to general receipts into the treasury.

A Second Crisis.

From 1840 to 1850, the whole Institution was very much depressed. It possessed a large amount of property, but it was mainly in land. Its value was not less than $100,000, as has been proven by subsequent sales; and though every expedient had been tried to make it productive, the most that could be realized from it was about $1,500 per annum. Of this sum, $900 per annum were required to pay interest, and $500 for taxes. Rents were accruing to the amount of about $1,200 yearly, on dwellings owned by the Institution. But on buildings that had stood fifteen or twenty years, a large part of the rents would be required in repairs.

In a financial condition so depressed, with Professors the fewest possible, and those on half pay, very tardily received, it is no wonder that students were few, and that the streams of benevolence that had so often watered Kenyon, were nearly dried up. The present writer, in asking for aid at one time, was told in effect, "You have a plenty of land, use that." The hint was taken, and the matter of a sale urged as the only possible hope of relief. This measure was first recommended by the Faculty, and then, after mature deliberation, by the Convention of Ohio; and very soon after 1850, nearly half of the land was sold.

Now a brighter day dawned upon Kenyon. The debt was paid off, credit restored, and the officers were promptly paid; so that the best talents the country afforded could now be commanded for Kenyon College. President Andrews was soon after appointed, who has no superior in ability to conduct an institution of learning, and so to adapt it to the wants of the country, as to command and deserve an extensive patronage.

Fears have sometimes been expressed, that the College is overshadowing the Theological Seminary. But present results prove conclusively, that the life of the College and Preparatory School is the life of the Theological Seminary. Through these there ever has, and probably ever will, come the main supply of candidates for the ministry, and, consequently, of students for the Seminary. The interests of both are identical, and what aids one will benefit the other.

From the very time of a change of the property of the Seminary, from an unproductive to a productive form, confidence and kind feeling toward it have been increasing.

Dr. Muenscher had little difficulty in selling scholarships to the amount of nearly $12,000. This was, doubtless, a judicious move, as it aided in bringing in students when they were most needed.

The year 1851 brought another favorable token. The Rev. G. T. Brooke, D. D., was appointed agent to solicit funds for a new Professorship. He entered upon his work, and had proceeded so far as to obtain the following donations:

Rev. E. H. Canfield, D. D., New York. $100
Hon. D. K. Este, Cincinnati.. 100
R. H. Marshall, Esq... 100
W. W. Corcoran, Esq., Washington City.......................... 100
A lady, Frederick, Md.. 100
Christ Church, Baltimore.. 100
Mr. Bash,   "   100
Mr. Carrol,   "   25

At this point the agent was most unexpectedly arrested in his course, and an end was put to his further solicitations. Here was a "new thing under the sun," at least for Kenyon. In the Theological Seminary at Alexandria, (a noble rival to that in Ohio, in the cause of Evangelical truth,) was a gentle and somewhat retiring young man, himself a student, by the name of Archibald Morrison. This young man encountered the agent with a spirit which our persevering friend, Dr. Brooke, was unprepared to resist, and in a very unobtrusive way, gave the whole sum of $10,000, and thus founded the *Griswold Professorship* in the Theological Seminary of the Diocese of Ohio.

The impulse now given to the Seminary, of which the above was both an evidence and a cause, made it necessary to provide additional rooms for Theological students. This want was met by the effort to complete the remaining half of Bexley Hall. The following list will show whence the funds for this purpose were derived:

Rt. Rev. C. P. McIlvaine, D. D. D. C. L.	$150	Rev. C. S. Doolittle, Granville,	$25
Rev. Dr. Burr, Portsmouth....	100	Rev. W. H. Nicholson, D. D., Cincinnati	50
Charles B. Goddard, Esq., Zanesville.	75	Rev. L. Burton, Cleveland.....	50
J. B. McKennon, Esq., Browns-ville, Pa.	50	N. G. Pendleton, Esq., Cin'a..	50
Thomas Sparrow, Esq., Colum-bus, O.	50	C. Newman, Esq., Norwalk...	25
A. H. Moss, Esq., Sandusky...	50	Rev. R. Taylor, Mt. Vernon...	6
G. W. Adams, Esq., Dresden..	50	W. Procter, Esq., Cincinnati...	25
Rev. G. W. Dubois, Chillicothe,	50	Harcourt Parish, Gambier.....	25
G. W. Jackson, Esq., Ironton,	50	St. Paul's Church, Chillicothe,	50
Prof. F. Wharton, Gambier...	50	Rev. C. W. Ferns, Circleville,	25
		Hon. C. Delano, Mt. Vernon...	50
		Hon. William Jay, New York,	100

This sum, last mentioned, was given some time before the rest, to fit up a room for a very worthy colored student, who has lately taken orders.

The following sums have also been given, at various times, to furnish rooms in Bexley Hall; the room being named from the source whence its furniture was supplied.

NAMES OF ROOMS IN BEXLEY HALL.

Ascension, N. Y.	$150	Bishop McIlvaine.	125
St. Paul's, Boston....	125	Carus.	125
Christ Church, Cincinnati....	150	John Farr.	125
St. Mark's, N. Y.	150	Pierrpont	125
St. George's, N. Y.	125		

The funds for the last four were solicited from various sources by Mrs. McIlvaine.

In the course of this gratifying progress, there was an equally increasing demand for funds; and as this demand increased more rapidly than the supply, extraordinary efforts were made by the Trustees themselves to make up the deficiency. The following will show the self-sacrifice of the Trustees, and members of the Convention, in order to make the income meet the expenses of the Institution.

Donations for this purpose were often made at meetings of the Board, and once in Convention, as follows:

Rev. Mr. Kellogg	$25	Rev. Dr. Claxton, and St.	
Platt Benedict, Esq	25	Paul's, Cleveland	$150
Richard Lane	5	S. Patrick, Esq	25
Bishop McIlvaine	390	Trinity Church, Lyme	10
Rev. Dr. Wing	50	A. Cunningham	9 75
Rev. Dr. Butler, for himself		Hon. W. H. Canfield	25
and Christ Church	575	Trinity Church, Columbus	50
Dr. Coleman, Troy	25	Harcourt Parish, Gambier	75
Warren Munger, Esq., Dayton	25	Rev. Dr. Smith	25
M. M. Granger, Esq., Zanes-		Swan & Andrews	55
ville	50	Rev. Mr. Maybin	20
E. E. Filmore, Esq., Zanesville	25	President Andrews	100
Rev. Mr. Blackaller	20	Rev. S. A. Bronson (previous	
Rev. A. Blake	25	to 1850)	600
Rev. J. McElroy, and St. Pe-			
ter's, Delaware	186		$2,598 75
Rev. Dr. Brooke	25		

ASCENSION HALL, AND NEW PROFESSORSHIPS.

About the year 1855, it became evident that increased accommodations would soon be needed for College students. This was deemed a just ground of applications for friendly aid from abroad. With the demand for more room, also arose a demand for an increase of Professors. To obtain such aid, and meet these demands, Bishop McIlvaine issued the following

STATEMENT AND APPEAL IN BEHALF OF KENYON COLLEGE.

BISHOP MCILVAINE solicits the kind attention of his friends, and all who desire the extension of our Church in the West, to the following respectful appeal and statement. It is in behalf of Kenyon College, situated at Gambier, Ohio, under Trustees appointed by the Convention of that Diocese, and devoted to the promotion of Christian Education, and more especially to that of candidates for the ministry, in the Episcopal Church. For convenience-sake, we here speak of the College and connected Theological Seminary, both of them at Gambier, and essentially united under the same Trustees and incorporation, under the one name of Kenyon College; because, although the corporate name is "Theological Seminary of the Diocese of Ohio," the other is the name most familiar to the public.

It is not to deliver this institution from debt, that aid is now sought. There

ASCENSION HALL

Wm. Tinsley Archt.

Middleton, Strobridge & Co. Lithos. Cin. O.

is no debt. But there is an unprecedented prosperity, and hence arises the present necessity. The present accommodations are so occupied with students, that there is room for only a very few more. The number of *undergraduates* is between one hundred and forty and one hundred and fifty. It is a remarkable and cheering fact, that of that number *seventy-seven* are communicants, forty of whom are preparing to enter, when they graduate, on theological study for the ministry, while there is reason to expect that of the remainder, many will make up their minds in the same direction. In these times of need as to laborers in God's vineyard, how encouraging and important these facts.

Never before has Kenyon College been the object of so much attention, East and West, as an institution to be relied on by the members of our Church for the education of their sons. Never has there been so strong and wide a feeling, among clergy and laity, that Kenyon College, however local and diocesan as to its control, is *national* as to its importance, and the usefulness to be expected from it, and the interest that should center upon it. In truth, the importance of that institution to the whole Church is measured only by that of having an evangelical ministry of our Church extended far and wide over all the States and Territories of the West. And hence the feeling is becoming very strong, that there is no object, connected with our duty as a Church, which should more engage the regard and liberal gifts of our people than the strengthening and enlargement of the facilities of Kenyon College, to place it on such a footing, as to adequate number of professors, accommodations for students, and the various means and conveniences for instruction, in all branches, that it may fully occupy the place to which it is called in the providence of God, that it may meet, satisfy, and retain, instead of disappointing and causing to react, the present incoming of public favor and expectation.

Then, what does Kenyon College need? We answer, *Means of enlargement.* In what?

First. In the number of its professorships.

It needs endowment for two professorships—one in the Theological Department; the other in the *Undergraduate Course.* It takes all the increase of income which the Trustees have been able to make, to meet the great increase which a few years have made in the cost of living, and consequently in the cost of supporting the instruction of the Institution on its old footing, as to the number of professors, etc. It has no income beyond its annual expenses. Enlargement, however demanded, is out of the question, without assistance. We ask, therefore, for aid at the hands of our brethren, in the endowment of two professorships, at a salary of $1,000 each, which, at 7 per cent., requires for each the sum of $15,000.

Secondly. Enlargement *in buildings.*

We need an additional building for the accommodation of more students. Scarcely any increase of students can now be received, while much is now promised, and much more is confidently expected.

We need another building for all the public purposes of the College, containing a suitable chapel for *daily* morning and evening prayers (the present place for such a purpose being unsuitable in the extreme); containing, also, accommodations for a chemical laboratory, for a philosophical cabinet and lectures, and rooms for all recitations and lectures. At present these objects are provided for most inconveniently and defectively, to the great detriment of the reputation of the Institution, and contraction of its usefulness.

Thirdly. Enlargement *as to means of instruction.*

Suitable apparatus for instruction in Chemistry, in Natural Philosophy, and other departments of physical science, is absolutely needed.

Fourthly. The means of providing residences for two professors.

All these objects, on a moderate estimate, will require from $65,000 to $70,000—an amount not great compared with the magnitude and permanence of the end to be attained—not great compared with what is readily raised by our brethren of other Christian churches in this country, for the seminaries and colleges under their control.

Without multiplying words, the undersigned respectfully seeks of his brethren of the laity the means of accomplishing the objects above specified. What better thing can be done for our Church extension, and our great work of thereby promoting the advancement of the Gospel, by means of the labors of an educated and faithful ministry? What better can be done by the East for the vast outspreading of the West, and its rapid growth of population; what better for the glory of God and the good of man? The undersigned is the more bold to ask this aid, because in having given himself (and for many years under most heavy burdens of difficulty and anxiety,) to the same cause, he has not omitted to take a larger share of its service than he asks now of any of his brethren. Those who are so kind as to be ready to help, can transmit to the undersigned, at Cincinnati, by mail, or can make their Rector their agent for that purpose—making their own terms of payment, provided that the time, as to individual subscriptions, be not over three years from date.

CHARLES P. McILVAINE,
Bishop of the Diocese of Ohio.

Nov. 15, 1856.

This statement and appeal met with the following response:

1. To erect a new college edifice, called *Ascension Hall*, these sums were subscribed, embracing the effort for building, and that for completing the north half:

Mrs. C. A. Spencer, St. George's, N. Y. $3000

Mr. James Sheafe, N. Y. ....1500.

Mr. John D. Wolfe, Grace Ch., N. Y. 500

Stewart Brown, Grace Church, N. Y. 500

James M. Brown, Ch. of Ascension..................................$200

E. H. Gillilan, Ch. of Ascension......................... 200

Aspinwall, Ch. of Ascension... 100

Schell................................ 100

Rev. Mr. Kellogg, Ohio......... 50

Rev. Peter Neff, jr...............$200
Rev. G. T. Bedell, D. D. 100
Capt. J. Strader.................. 100
Capt. Dupont, Delaware.. 200
J. B. McKennon, Brownsville,
Pa. 50
Miss H. B. H., by Dr. Bedell... 200
R. B. Bowler, Cin., O........... 100
J. W. Andrews and others,
Columbus, O.................... 85
G. Taylor........................ 100
Mr. Corcoran, Wash., D. C..... 200

Theodore Brown, St.Matthew's
P. O., Ky........................ $25
John Bohlen, Phila............. 200
Miss C. M. Bohlen, Phila...... 200
Mrs. H. R. Huchinson, N. Y.... 200
J. W. Brown, Mt. Holly, N. J. 100
Ladies, St. Paul's, Boston...... 137
Mr. Probasco, Cin., per Bp. M. 200
Mr. Barclay, of N. Y., appli-
cable to this...................1000
A young lady, N. Y., appli-
cable to this 1000

2. To erect a library building, to be called *St. George's Hall*, St. George's Church has given $3,282.50, to be increased to $10,000 when the Trustees are ready to proceed with the building.

3. To found two professorships. One was commenced in New York, for which the following sums were subscribed:

A member of St. Mark's......$1000
A lady,   "   250
A communicant "   50
A lady......... 25
E. W. Cunningham, Brooklyn.1000
Nicholas Luquier...............1000
Charles Congreve................ 500
Sydney Corbett. 200
Lewis Morris, Chr. Church.... 150
Thomas D. Middleton............ 150
Mrs. Minturn.................. 50
George Merle.................. 25
E. H. Hand...................... 25
A. E. Masters................... 50

Editors and Publishers Prot.
Churchman $16
—— Stanton. 100
—— Townsend 50
John N. Taylor. 100
H. G. R. N. Fisher 75
Carter & Brothers (Library).. 100
Mr. Schafter, Chr. Church...... 200
Mr. Butler and lady........... 150
Mr. John Halley............... 500
Mr. Ersene....................... 500
Mr. Thomas Messenger.......... 300
Mr. Peet....................... 200

Another professorship, named *Bedell*, in honor of the late Dr. Bedell, of St. Andrew's, was started in Philadelphia, and met with the following success:

Thomas H. Powers............$1000
Jay Cook.....................1000
Joseph Harrison.............1000
John Bohlen and sister.........1000
Lewis R. Ashurst......... 300
John W. Thomas................. 300
W. H. Ashurst.................. 300
John D. Taylor................. 300
A. Whitney & Sons............. 300
R. G. Stolesbury............... 150
F. Wharton.................... 300
Lemuel Coffin 100
J. H. Hildeburn................. 100
L. Montgomery Bond........... 100
Aug. Heaton................... 100
J. McCutchin.................. 100
J. W. Thomas.................. 100

Joseph A. Clay................... $90
A. E. Ashburn................... 75
Isaac Norris 60
John Hockley.................. 60
Vin. L. Bradford............... 60
John Grigg................... 100
C. B. Darborrow 50
J. A. Hasman................ 50
J. B. Vandusen 50
George Clay..... 50
J. Clarke Cooke............... 15
Ed. Olmsted.................. 30
Mrs. R. Gimbes............... 50
Mr. Comegys.................. 10
W. Hanby.................... 15
Miss S. Goodfellow............ 3
W. H. Seal.................. 25

W. P. Hinds.....................\$ 25	H. C. Howard......................\$ 6
Mrs. Marshall...................... 3	Miss Grisley....................... 6
S. A. Brooks....................... 3	Cash subscriptions paid......... 137 50
Mrs. ———........................ 3	

Of the last above, to this date, July 1, 1860, the sum of \$4407.-84 has been paid.

When the above subscriptions had progressed thus far, another most agreeable surprise occurred.

Mr. J. D. Wolfe and wife, and Mrs. Spencer, the sister of Mrs. W., of West Chester, N. Y., whose names the reader of this will find oft repeated in this record, and whose venerable father, just before his decease, gave \$6000 to the Bishop of Ohio, for the benefit of aged and infirm clergymen, in this diocese, unitedly founded a professorship in Kenyon College, giving, together, \$16,000. This was accordingly named by the Trustees, the *Lorillard & Wolfe Professorship*.

Nearly at the same time with these expressions of good will, the benevolent John Johns, of Baltimore County, M. D., departed this life. His name, too, was often on the subscription lists for Kenyon College, and in his will, through the special good offices of the late lamented Dr. Johns, he made the generous bequest to the Institution of \$15,000. This came not as a result, but among the results of the "Statement and Appeal" issued November, 1856.

They will, therefore, sum up as follows:

Donation to St. George's Hall..\$ 3,282 50
Ascension Hall Subscription.. 10,252 00
Toward a New York Professorship.................................. 6,666 00
Toward Bedell Professorship, collected 1860.................. 4,407 00
The Lorillard & Wolfe Professorship............................. 15,000 00
The Johns' Legacy.. 15,000 00
\$54,607 50

All the above Professorship subscriptions are not yet collected, but enough has been realized to enable the Institution to establish two professorships, and proceed with Ascension Hall so far that we have assurances it will be completed by the Church of the Ascension, N. Y.

THE STRONG SCHOLARSHIP FUND.

The Rev. E. A. Strong has, by permission of the Trustees, solicited scholarships of \$200 each, for the exclusive benefit of young men studying for the ministry. The sum of $8,331 has been received in this way, which, when it shall reach a certain amount, is to be regarded as a foundation for a professorship. This, and the Muenscher scholarship funds, together, amount to $13,931. These, it is to be remembered, are not donations, but loans, on which a high interest is paid in the shape of tuition.

RECAPITULATION.

Received through Bishop Chase	$ 64,000 00
Collected at the East in 1833, through Bishop McIlvaine	26,600 00
Temporary Professorship, 1833	1,220 00
Collected by Dr. Sparrow, in Ohio	5,341 00
Collected for Bishop's House, in 1832	609 00
Bexley Hall Collection in England	12,370 07
Collection to same endowment in 1843	35,000 00
Compromise of Scholarships	503 33
Griswold Professorship	10,725 00
Clarke & H. More Scholarships	2,276 55
Different collections for Bexley Hall	2,256 00
Mrs. Davis' Legacy	510 00
Additions to Milnor Professorship by St. George's Church	2,500 00
Collections for deficiencies	2,598 00
Answer to Statement and Appeal	54,607 50
Muenscher & Strong Scholarship funds	13,931 00
	$235,047 45

In reference to the above, the donors will of right ask what property and assets does the Institution now possess, to show that these funds have been judiciously expended. To this it may be said, in answer :

1. Temporary buildings and improvements, that cost, at different times, upwards of $17,000, have long since passed away. They have been used up for the purposes intended, and have doubtless been worth, to the Church and the world, all they cost. Much also has been expended in the repairs of buildings in the course of 30 years, that can not now be included in their present value. Should it be estimated, therefore, that $20,000 have been absorbed in this

way, and the statement be allowed the benefit of this deduction, it would be but fair and just. But this is not necessary.

2. Abundant assets in real estate and vested funds remain on hand to more than equal in value every dollar that has been given to the Institution.

The following statement, carefully prepared by a committee appointed for the purpose, is an estimate of the present value of the property of the Board:

Kenyon College.	$ 35,000	00
Rosse Chapel..	13,335	00
Bexley Hall..	17,195	00
Milnor Hall........	7,000	00
Ascension Hall...................................	30,450	00
Professors' Houses.............	17,500	00
Other Dwellings...................................	1,500	00
Lands, valued at...................................	73,000	00
Vested Funds, including the Milnor Fund...	88,000	00
	$282,980	00
Deduct Donations,............	235,047	45
Balance ....$	47,932	55

One person, to whom the public are especially indebted for the safe keeping and accumulation of the funds of Kenyon College, ought here to be especially noted, viz: the Rev. Dr. Wing. During the greater part of the time, for thirty years, in addition to the duties of a Professorship in the Seminary, he has been general and financial agent, and book-keeper. Through him, at different times, have been sold more than 7,000 acres of land, and not much less than $100,000 have been expended in buildings under his direction. The management of the whole concern has, in fact, rested on his shoulders, and it is but just that in this Report the Trustees should emphatically say, "Well done, good and faithful servant."

In conclusion, let it be said, in behalf of the Trustees, Officers and Students, who have, during a third of a century past, been connected with our Diocesan Institution at Gambier, in the name of the many souls that have here been born again, and are now rejoicing in Heaven: in the name of the many churches whose pulpits have been filled with Gospel preachers from this Institution: in the name of the millions yet to inhabit the valley of the Ohio, who shall look up to Kenyon as the Cambridge or Oxford of the West, in tones of warmest thanks, may Heaven's richest blessing rest upon every donor. Honor to the poor man, woman or child, that has given a dime, as well as the rich who have given their thousands. The donor to this Institution who has given, or shall give or bequeath, for its advancement, what God has blessed him with here, but which he can not carry with him, will have built a monument more durable than marble or brass, a monument that will make his name loved as well as admired.

N. B. In the course of thirty years many subscription-lists have been lost, and while the amounts were carefully retained on the books, at Gambier, the names of the donors have been lost sight of. If this Statement shall fall into the hands of any who can supply any instances of this kind, the Trustees will be grateful for the information.

AN EXTRACT

FROM THE WESTERN EPISCOPALIAN, OCT. 4, 1860.

THE Theological Department has sent forth ninety-one Ministers of the Gospel, during the twenty-five years since its organization.

Two hundred and seventy-six young men have graduated from Kenyon College during the thirty-three years since its foundation, of whom ninety have become Ministers of the Gospel.

It may safely be said that not less than one hundred and fifty who have been students in these Institutions, have entered the ministry. Such a work have they done for the Church, though yet in their infancy, and heretofore struggling with the difficulties incident to a new enterprise in a new country. But Kenyon College has done more than educate pious young men, who have become students in her various classes. By the blessing of God, many who commenced their course of pupilage here, unconcerned about the things of eternity, have gone forth into the world faithful, devoted Christian men; some to preach the Gospel of Christ in this or foreign lands; and others to labor for the same good cause as earnest, zealous laymen. During the last six years, ninety-seven students have graduated from Kenyon College; of these, sixty-seven were communicants; thirty-two have entered upon the work of the ministry, or are candidates for orders, and thirty-six, by the converting power of the Holy Spirit, as we trust, were brought into the Church here. During the same time, including those who have not graduated, fifty-nine students have become communicants while connected with the Institution.

At the present writing, there are one hundred and ninety-four students in all the departments of the Institution, of whom ninety-four are communicants, and seventy are studying with a view to the ministry in our Church.

The facts presented above speak for themselves, and show that God has blessed these Institutions by the converting influences of the Holy Spirit;

and that He continues to own and sanctify the means employed to develop the minds and cultivate the hearts of the youth here assembled.

The young Christian here enjoys many privileges to promote the growth of grace in his own heart, and many opportunities to labor for the cause of Christ. He is beyond the reach of many of the seductive influences of worldly amusements and fashionable vices; he resides in a community made up almost entirely of members of our Church; he has the association and sympathy of about one hundred young Christians, who, like himself, are students in the Institution; he is required to attend the full Morning and Evening Service, and hear two evangelical sermons each Sunday in Rosse Chapel; he is invited to unite in the Service and listen to a Lecture each Thursday evening; on each Tuesday evening the officers and students of the Theological Seminary hold a Social Prayer Meeting in Bexley Hall; the officers and students of the College meet for the same purpose in Ascension Hall, and the officers and students of the Grammar School, in Milnor Hall; and in addition to these, each class in College has its own Prayer Meeting on Friday evening.

Lightning Source UK Ltd.
Milton Keynes UK
UKHW020213030119
334668UK00005B/308/P